Andrea Pal-Liebscher

English for Civil Engineers

Bibliografische Information der Deutschen Nationalbibliothek: Die Deutsche Nationalbibliothek verzeichnet diese Publikation in der Deutschen Nationalbibliografie; detaillierte bibliografische Daten sind im Internet über http://dnb.dnb.de abrufbar.

©2019 Pal-Liebscher, Andrea

Herstellung und Verlag: BoD – Books on Demand, Norderstedt

ISBN: 9783749470792

Preface

This book has been written for learners of English who are working or studying in the field of Civil Engineering. For successful completion of this course, learners are recommended to have B1-level (CEFR) English language competence or higher. The course will help learners consolidate their English skills at B2 level while dealing with job-related topics, with special focus on vocabulary enhancement and the appropriate application of terms in those areas. The technical readings, creative activities and grammar tasks embedded in context serve the purpose of improving the reading, speaking and writing skills in the first place. The supplementary grammar exercises added to the general course material will provide language learners the opportunity to further improve their grammar awareness and accuracy.

Acknowledgements

I am grateful to my colleagues in the Language Center and in the Department of Architecture and Civil Engineering of the RheinMain University of Applied Sciences in Germany who have always supported my work with useful comments and suggestions.

A very special thanks to Julia Hartley whose expertise in teaching English for Civil Engineers, genuine motivation and perseverance in offering efficient language classes for academic purposes greatly inspired my work. I would never have been able to write this course book without our discussions and without the civil engineering course materials we compiled together in the past.

I would also like to thank my husband who always knows how to tackle computer problems in a fast and efficient way and patiently explained the nitty-gritty of document formatting along the way.

Table of content

TOPIC 1
Main areas of civil engineering

This topic focuses on:

◊ What civil engineering is

◊ What civil engineers do

◊ What skills and qualities they need

◊ The main areas in which a civil engineer can work

◊ Grammar:

- The use of modal verbs

- Word formations

Responsibilities of a civil engineer

When we think about the term "civil engineering", we often associate it with the world's most magnificent constructions like the Burj Khalifa in Dubai, the Shard in London or the Three Gorges Dam in China. A major part of civil engineering is indeed about designing safe structures and **overseeing** the construction process. It belongs to the main tasks of a civil engineer to **carry out** feasibility studies, do structural calculations, organize the purchase and delivery of materials and building equipment. Civil engineers also have to **manage** budgets and, in general, **make sure** that the project runs smoothly and is completed on time and within the given budget. They meet clients, architects and subcontractors, **discuss** various aspects of the construction project and **resolve** conflicts that arise along the way.

Besides the actual construction of different types of buildings, civil engineering is also about **maintaining** the infrastructure that we depend on every day: our transportation systems (roads, railways, subways, bridges and tunnels); our energy and water supplies; our waste treatment and flood control systems. Civil engineers have to **keep** this infrastructure running and **improve** it to meet new challenges, such as population growth, climate change and natural disasters.

Further to creating and maintaining the infrastructure that is essential to modern life, civil engineers in certain areas are also responsible for creating a healthy habitat and ecosystems around us, **seeking** ways to make sure that we live in harmony with nature. Expanding urban areas and preserving natural habitats at the same time is often a challenging task. Therefore, civil engineers have to be able to offer and **implement** solutions to complex problems. Simply put, civil engineers play a significant role in various different aspects of our lives. They shape our world.

Civil engineering is a challenging profession. Generally speaking, all civil engineers are **required** to be innovative individuals with good analytical and logical thinking skills. To be successful, they need a problem-solving mind, the ability to understand the bigger picture and also the willingness to **collaborate** with a number of other professionals.

Task 1: Match the following verbs with the most adequate nouns / expressions, using each of them only once. When finished, make sentences on your own using these collocations

1.	purchase	a.	studies
2.	shape	b.	calculations
3.	oversee	c.	materials
4.	carry out	d.	conflicts
5.	meet	e.	new challenges
6.	live	f.	in harmony with nature
7.	maintain	g.	the infrastructure
8.	resolve	h.	the workers on site
9.	implement	i.	solutions to problems
10.	do	j.	the world

1. ____   2. ____   3. ____   4. ____   5. ____   6. ____   7. ____   8. ____   9. ____   10. ____

Task 2: Consider the importance of the following skills and qualities for a civil engineer and write them in the appropriate table.

have good analytical skills   have attention to detail   be athletic
be married   be good at mathematics   be messy
be good at multitasking   be a non-smoker   be well-groomed
have good problem-solving skills   have a creative mind   be impatient
have stamina   speak foreign languages   be a team player

essential (= a must)	quite useful (= an asset)	unimportant / irrelevant	negative / unacceptable

Task 3: Now complete the following sentences choosing skills / qualities from your table.

Civil engineers must   ....

They may / should also ....

They don't have to ....

They mustn't ....

Task 4. Use <u>the past forms</u> of the modal verbs in the following sentences.

1. The structural engineer ……………………………………….. (must) finish some complex structural calculations before going home last night.

2. The client ……………………………. (can not) come to the meeting last week because he was away on business.

3. The students ……………………………………………. (mustn't) enter the construction site without wearing helmets when they visited the site yesterday.

4. The structural engineer ………………………………………….. (not have to) call the client as he managed to come over to his office.

5. The construction manager was glad to see that the workers …………………………………….. (can) dig the holes much faster with the new wide-bucket excavator.

Main areas of civil engineering

Structural engineering

Meanwhile architects design building based on what the client has envisioned, it is the job of a structural engineer to **check if** the implementation of the plans is really realistic, in other words, if the construction is feasible. They must **consider** aesthetics, structural stability, construction costs and sustainability at the same time, while also **ensuring** that the construction is serviceable, which means that it successfully **fulfills** the function it is designed for. Sometimes structural engineers and architects work in close cooperation to create the final design plans so that the project can be **completed** successfully and the result lives up to the expectations.

Structural engineers are responsible for the physical integrity of various different types of constructions such as buildings, bridges, dams, tunnels, flyovers or offshore oil platforms, among other things. They **identify and analyze** the loads which act upon a structure and the forces which arise within that structure when exposed to those loads. Their primary concern is to **ensure** safety and durability during the planned service period of the construction. Depending on the location, they may also need to make sure that the structure can withstand a force of nature like a strong earthquake.

Construction management / site engineering

Construction managers **are responsible for** the entire construction project from start to completion. They **arrange** the complicated "dirt dance" on the construction site: they **oversee** the construction workers who **execute** various tasks, such as mixing cement, pouring concrete, operating cranes and excavators. They **make sure** that the project is carried out effectively, on time and on budget.

Naturally, they have to be on the construction site on a regular basis and they often need to **solve** problems like how to get wet concrete from the ground to the top of a skyscraper before it hardens. In general, they must often consider which construction methods would be the most appropriate to use. Other functions of a construction engineer may include preparing and **interpreting** diagrams and charts, **monitoring** and **comparing** prices of suppliers, **implementing** project safety plans and carrying out surveys (e.g. of the soil condition and the ground water level for a construction project)

Materials engineering

Materials engineers deal with the properties and characteristics of materials. They **examine** the molecular structure of materials and try to change it in order to **improve** already existing building materials such as concrete, steel, brick, mortar or plastic.

Besides that, they also create new alloys by **combining** different metallic components and polymers (that is, chemical compounds) by creating various different chains of molecules. They make new composites that are lighter, cheaper, more elastic or more durable and also more sustainable. One of the newest technologies available to this engineering discipline is nanotechnology, which **enables** researchers to inspect the structure of materials at a billionth-of-a-meter scale.

Materials engineers may also **be involved in** environmental technology, by **developing** new ways of recycling materials. For instance, a materials scientist can develop methods to recycle non-metallic components of electric appliances which can then be re-used.

Geotechnical engineering

To make a building sturdy and safe, engineers need to determine if the soil beneath a future structure is suitable for supporting its foundation. This is a major task of a geotechnical engineer. They also need to evaluate potential hazards due to environmental impacts like landslides or flooding after heavy rains and earthquakes. They must guarantee that the structure to be built on a piece of land will be safe for the occupants and suitable for its planned use.

Geotechnical engineers do a lot of field work and sometimes they must get their hands dirty while studying the properties of rocks, soil and underground water as they **collect** the necessary facts about a building site. They advise construction engineers and help them choose an appropriate structural foundation that is durable and cost-effective.

Environmental engineering

The different structures (buildings, dams, roads and bridges) that are built around us may have a negative impact on the environment. It is the duty of environmental engineers to estimate those potential risks and plan ways to **limit** the harmful effects of constructions on the natural surroundings. They **identify** potential health risks and environmental damage, **evaluate** the significance of the hazard and **advise on** possible treatment (for example concerning the purification of contaminated sites).

Our consumer societies in the 21st century produce a lot of waste, most of which ends up on landfills. How we **manage** these sites and how we **dispose of** electronic scrap, nuclear waste and other types of hazardous materials, belongs to the scope of environmental engineering, as well as **developing** ways of recycling.

Environmental engineers might also work on a more global scale. Among other things, they **study** methods to **minimize** the effects of acid rain, **reduce** global warming and **limit** automobile emissions.

Water resources engineering

You turn on the tap at home and out comes water. It's clean, safe and it's in every building. Making sure people have clean drinking water in their homes is one of the most important responsibilities of water resources engineers.

They design sewage systems and water treatment plants for the drinking water supply systems and they also organize and manage the placement of pipelines. In addition, they may **be involved in** flood control projects and the **mapping out** of drainage systems for **dealing with** water flow in case of excess water.

Surveying and mapping

Surveying is one of the oldest civil engineering disciplines. It dates back to the ancient Egyptians who used it to **divide** land into plots more than 3000 years ago. Today, surveying the land is essential before construction work can begin on a building site. Accurate legal boundaries for property ownership **require** exact measurements, which is **provided** by the surveying technicians.

Our automobile navigation systems would be unimaginable without the thorough work of surveying and mapping engineers. They **determine** the position of natural and man-made objects, **measure** distances, extensions, elevations and they also **document** the collected data. Together with cartographers, they create maps of the Earth's surface and update those maps by re-setting boundaries if changes take place. They use highly sophisticated techniques (e.g. satellite imagery and aerial photography) to **provide** views of the Earth from above for digital maps.

Transportation engineering

Transportation engineering is concerned with the efficient and safe movement of people and goods. It involves planning, designing, constructing, and maintaining transportation infrastructure such as streets, canals, highways, railroads, airports, harbors, and public transportation systems, such as trams, subways, buses.

With the development of new Intelligent Transportation Systems (ITS), transport engineers use state-of-the-art computer tools to **provide** fast and accurate traffic information for travelers and advanced traffic control options for the operators of vehicles.

Besides dealing with the already existing infrastructure, they also **model** traffic scenarios that help them **evaluate** potential future impacts of new developments. Besides that, they can also **simulate** current traffic scenarios to **figure out** efficient ways of dealing with the existing problems.

Urban planning & development

Urban planners try to create sustainable urban environments with long-lasting structures, buildings and optimal 'liveability' for their inhabitants. Their primary concern is to **make sure** that the community lives in harmony with itself and the natural environment that surrounds it.

They focus on reducing negative environmental impacts (e.g. harmful emissions from traffic) by changing the built environment to create smart cities which, among other things, support sustainable transport. Their goal is to design compact urban neighborhoods whose residents need **to commute** much less than the residents of some metropolitan areas with their crawling suburbs.

Forensic engineering

When a man-made construction (a house, a bridge, a roadway or a dam) collapses, it can have different reasons: inappropriate use, faulty construction, data miscalculation, material failure (or a combination of these factors), force of nature or even a criminal act. It is the job of a forensic engineer to **investigate** the circumstances of the collapse, **determine** the cause of failure and find out if someone must be held accountable.

People often call forensic engineering "reverse engineering". Basically, it isn't about creating something new. It is much more about tracing back the past: they **interview** members of the design team, check structural plans, **analyze** debris in order to **figure out** what may have gone wrong.

Forensic engineers often work together with law enforcement officers. Occasionally, they also have to **testify** at court as an expert witness, **presenting** potential evidence that may **impact** court decisions.

Task 1: Fill in the missing verbs. Choose the verb that is the most suitable.

1. In different areas of civil engineering, the engineers must _____ several area-specific tasks.
a) work with   b) deal   c) carry out   d) involve

2. A structural engineer, for example, needs to _____ loads and forces that act on a structure.
a) provide   b) ensure   c) look for   d) identify

3. Construction managers _____ workers on the building site.
a) execute   b) oversee   c) investigate   d) estimate

4. A materials engineer _____ the components of materials and their characteristics.
a) examines   b) deals   c) carries out   d) guarantees

5. A materials engineer also tries to _____ existing building materials (so that they become better).
a) inspect   b) identify   c) ensure   d) improve

6. A surveyor _____ distances between plots so that the legal boundaries of properties can be determined.
a) executes   b) measures   c) maintains   d) arranges

7. A forensic engineer, together with law enforcement officers, tries to _____ the cause of a building collapse.
a) commission   b) require   c) determine   d) resolve

8. A transportation engineer _____ the public transportation system.
a) carries out   b) maintains   c) inspects   d) compares

9. A geotechnical engineer _____ the rock and soil under the ground.
a) maintains   b) determines   c) examines   d) provides

10. It is an important duty of an urban planner to _____ a community's land use.
a) optimize   b) anticipate   c) investigate   d) compare

Task 2: Compare the following jobs based on the aspects below. Find similarities and differences.

- the working environment
- main tasks
- necessary skills

1. structural engineer – construction manager

2. environmental engineer – urban planner

3. material engineer – forensic engineer

4. surveyor – transportation engineer

5. geotechnical engineer – water resources engineer

Task 3: Fill in the table by adding the noun forms of the verbs on the left

Verb	Noun	Verb	Noun
challenge		consider	
maintain		assess	
support		evaluate	
improve		research	
analyze		develop	
discuss		use	
treat		advise	
deliver		protect	
complete		compare	
grow		identify	
document		measure	
invest		commute	
implement		require	
respond		study	
limit		manage	
apply		calculate	
increase		decrease	
choose		mix	

Task 4: Fill in the missing words in the following sentences. Your sentence must have the same meaning as the original sentence.

1. The population is growing rapidly in urban areas.
   There is a rapid population ……………………………………… in urban areas.
2. It is expensive to maintain the infrastructure properly in metropolitan areas.
   Proper ……………………………………… of the infrastructure is expensive in metropolitan areas.
3. Please consider this option.
   Please take this option into …………………………………………….
4. If wood is treated properly, it is protected against humidity.
   Proper ……………………………………… of wood provides …………………………… against humidity.
5. They delivered the goods on time.
   The ………………………………….. of the goods was arranged on time.
6. When is the foundation expected to be completed?
   When can we expect ………………………….…………… of the foundation?
7. The materials scientist analyzes the chemical properties of composite materials thoroughly.
   The materials scientist provides a thorough …………………………………… of the composite materials.
8. Surveyors have to measure the property boundaries very precisely.
   Concerning property boundaries, precise …………………………………… done by surveyors are a must.
9. The construction manager has documented each and every step of the building process.
   The construction manager has kept a detailed ……………………………………… of the building process.
10. Environmental engineers make sure that the natural habitat of endangered animals is protected.
    The ……………………………………. of the natural habitat of endangered animals belongs to the scope of environmental engineering.
11. The manual describes how to use the device properly.
    Proper ……………………………… of the device is described in the manual.
12. The geotechnical engineer has already assessed the properties of the planned construction site.
    The ……………………………… of the planned construction site has already been completed by the geotechnical engineer.
13. The city council has to invest a lot of money so that they can further develop the socially deprived parts of the city.
    Financial …………………………… for the further ……………………………… of the socially deprived parts of the city must be considered by the city council.
14. Property prices have significantly increased recently.
    There has been a significant ………………………………….. in property prices recently.
15. People living in suburbs must commute very long distances sometimes.
    People living in suburbs must take very long ………………………………. into account sometimes.
16. If a coat of paint is applied on steel structures, they can be protected against rusting.
    The ……………………………… of a coat of paint can protect steel structures against rusting.
17. We never had any doubts that this unique roof design would be feasible.
    We never questioned the ……………………………………… of this unique roof design.
18. The applicant was able to solve problems quite well.
    The applicant had good problem solving …………………………………….

TOPIC 2
Loads, forces, building materials

This topic focuses on:

⬦ Loads that act on a structure

⬦ Forces that affect the structural integrity of a building

⬦ Mechanical properties of building materials

⬦ Common applications of building materials

⬦ Grammar:

- Comparisons

- Passive voice

- Adverbs and adjectives

Civil engineering basics

<u>Loads</u>

All structures must be able to withstand various different loads or they will fall apart. Structural load can be caused by gravity (which gives physical structures their weight) or it can have a dynamic source like wind flow, rainfall, snowfall, seismic tremors. If the loads acting on the structure exceed the **load bearing capacity** of the construction, it has a negative impact on the structure. The forces that are released when a structure is subjected to different loads can change the shape of structural components or of the entire construction.

The weight of the structure itself is called the **dead load**. The weight of anything or anyone on the structure (e.g. people or furniture in a house, vehicles on a bridge) is called the **live load**. In a hurricane, typhoon or tornado, a structure is exposed to very strong **wind load**. When a structure expands or shrinks with the change of temperature, it experiences **thermal load**. When the soil beneath a structure sinks unevenly, the structure is subjected to **settlement** problems. During an earthquake, the ground beneath a structure moves backwards and forwards due to **seismic tremors**, in other words, **earthquake load**.

Dead loads and live loads are vertical loads because they push downwards on a structure whereas **environmental loads** can be **vertical** (e.g. snow or rain) or **horizontal / lateral** (e.g. wind).

Environmental loads (wind, rain, snow, earthquake) are also called **dynamic loads** as they aren't always present and they vary in intensity. They are considered unpredictable sources because they can suddenly become very intense resulting in severe damage even to otherwise stable constructions.

<u>Forces</u>

When a structure is subjected to different loads, forces are released that have an impact on the shape and the integrity of the structural components (or of the entire structure).

- **Compression** causes the structure to be squeezed together. When it is squeezed, it tends to become shorter.
- **Tension** makes a material stretch. When a material is pulled apart, it tends to become longer.
- **Bending** occurs when a structure is subjected to compression from above and tension from below.
- **Shearing** is a force that causes parts of a structure to slide past one another in opposite directions.
- **Torsion** is the force that causes a structural member to twist about a longitudinal axis.

Forces cause deformation on the materials. If a material is quite flexible and it gets back to its original shape after the impact of a certain force, the structure experiences **elastic deformation**. If a material is more rigid and the structure does not gain back its original shape after the force is removed, the structure experiences permanent change due to **plastic deformation**.

<u>Application of civil engineering basics</u>

Since the different loads acting on the structure and the forces released during the interaction can greatly influence the stability of a construction, engineers must take into consideration the impact of these loads and forces prior to construction, during structural design. Factors that influence the design decisions include the anticipated use of the construction, the expected weather the structure will be exposed to, and the soil condition underneath the planned building. Besides structural design, engineers must choose the most suitable building materials under the given circumstances.

Task 1: Match the words on the left with the synonyms / short explanations on the right. Write the letter next to the number <u>below the box.</u>

1. tension	a. natural load
2. elastic deformation	b. squeezing
3. torsion	c. sinking
4. environmental load	d. permanent change
5. seismic tremors	e. twisting
6. shearing	f. shrinking and expanding by change of temperature
7. dead load	g. stretching
8. compression	h. furniture in a building
9. plastic deformation	i. sliding
10. settlement	j. temporary change
11. thermal load	k. earthquake load
12. live load	l. the weight of a structure

1. _____ 2. _____ 3. _____ 4. _____ 5. _____ 6. _____ 7. _____ 8. _____ 9. _____ 10. _____ 11. _____ 12. _____

Task 2: Put the following active sentences into passive.

1. Wind storms often destroy people's homes around the world.

   ....

2. Construction workers drove some piles into the ground.

   ....

3. The wind tore off the plywood planks that clad the building.

   ....

4. The falling tree crushed the roof of the building.

   ....

5. Engineers have recently investigated the cause of the collapse.

   ....

6. They have to make the construction site accessible for the cranes.

   ....

7. They took flood hazards into consideration when they made these houses.

   ....

Mechanical properties of building materials

Engineers must consider the mechanical properties of building materials in order to choose the most suitable materials for the different parts of the building construction. They must take into consideration how hard, soft, brittle, plastic, ductile or elastic a material is.

Hardness of a material is defined as the degree of a material's resistance to deformation (e.g. indentation, penetration or scratching). A hard material can resist the impact of another material. It is the *softer* material that undergoes deformation when two materials come into contact.

Elasticity refers to the property of a material to return to its original shape when the force is removed. Elastic materials keep their original form.

Plasticity means the opposite of elasticity. After the force no longer has an impact on the structure, the material stays in the altered shape. A plastic material doesn't return to its original shape.

Ductility can be described as the resistance of a material to break when subjected to bending or twisting. A ductile material will bend or twist, but it won't break easily when exposed to forces.

Brittleness is the opposite of ductility. It causes the material to break without warning. A brittle material doesn't undergo any plastic deformation. It breaks immediately when exposed to forces.

In addition to the above features, the **weight of a material** must also be considered carefully. Very heavy materials may increase the compression (due to large dead load) to an extent that exceeds the load bearing capacity of a construction. Light materials may have difficulties resisting tensile forces.

Task: Compare the following materials based on the <u>features described in the text above</u>. In your sentences, use the following forms:

- the base form of comparison (as … as … / not as … as …),
- the comparative form (…-er / more … than …)
- the superlative form (the …-est /the most …)

Examples: Wood is <u>lighter than</u> brick. Rubber is <u>the lightest</u> material.

diamond	rubber	glass	cast iron	aluminum	wood	brick

1. ....
2. ....
3. ....
4. ....
5. ....

The most common building materials

Concrete is made of water, cement and aggregate materials such as gravel or sand. It is a widely used construction material because of its low cost, flexibility, durability, and high compression strength. Furthermore, it has high resistance to fire. Meanwhile it is very strong in compression, it is quite weak in tension: it cracks easily when exposed to tensile forces and it has low thermal resistance (that is, it cracks with sudden changes of temperature). Another positive feature of concrete is its moldability. Liquid concrete can be molded to different shapes before it hardens.

Reinforced concrete is gained by pouring concrete over a gridwork of steel rods (so called reinforcement bars or "rebars" in short). In recent modern constructions, fiberglass is sometimes used to replace steel. These incorporated reinforcement components increase the tensile strength of the otherwise brittle material to a great extent, making reinforced concrete very strong in both compression and tension. The only disadvantages of reinforced concrete are the increased costs and the larger weight.

Cast iron is a very heavy and brittle material that contains approximately 95% iron and 5% carbon. Cast iron is very strong in compression but weak in tension. It has practically zero ductility, which means, it doesn't yield when exposed to tension. It breaks suddenly, without any prior cracks on the structure. Thus, unlike concrete buildings, cast iron constructions do not show small signs of damage. A positive feature of cast iron is that it retains high strength when exposed to heat. Although its melting point is relatively low, it can resist heat for a longer time period before undergoing larger deformations.

Steel is an iron alloy with a reduced level of carbon (it contains only 2% or less carbon). It is used very frequently in constructions because it is very strong in compression and tension, easily moldable to different shapes and lighter than some other alternatives (e.g. reinforced concrete). Steel is elastic until reaching yield (which refers to the point when it stops behaving elastically and starts to undergo permanent deformation). Beyond the yield point it becomes ductile. The traditional carbon steel has the disadvantage of having relatively low fire resistance, but modern steel alloys manifest an increased ability to withstand extreme heat. Being an iron derivate, steel rusts. To protect it against corrosion, steel is often used in construction as an alloy (e.g. by adding chromium and nickel to steel). Although being practically rust-free, **stainless steel** is much more expensive than steel, which is a great disadvantage if the construction costs must be kept within a reasonable budget. A much cheaper alternative is to apply a coat of paint or a spray on steel to protect it against corrosion.

Aluminium (BE) / Aluminum (AE) is a soft and lightweight material. Pure aluminum has a relatively low yield point, but aluminum alloys have a very high yield strength. Beyond yield it is a very ductile material. It is formed into different shapes quite easily and it has high compressive and tensile strength (as an alloy, with added components like magnesium and copper). Its resistance to corrosion depends on the added components, but basically it is fairly corrosion resistant. The disadvantage of aluminum is its price: high-quality aluminum alloys are rather expensive.

Brick is a frequently used building material for low-rise buildings due to its low price, high resistance to fire and attractive look (as compared to concrete which is rather unattractive). Since it is moderately strong in compression and weak in tension, it is not suitable for the construction of high-rise buildings. Like concrete, it can crack when it is under tension and also with sudden changes of temperature.

Wood / timber is one of the rare natural, biodegradable building materials. It has been used in building construction since ancient times (just like natural stones). Due to its sustainability, it is experiencing a revival in environmentally friendly construction design all over the world. In some areas (e.g. countries in Scandinavia) it has always belonged to the most preferred construction materials for low-rise buildings. Timber is moderately strong in compression and tension, but its strength basically depends on the type of wood. It has good insulation properties and provides healthy living conditions. The downside of using wood in constructions is that it swells when water penetrates into its structure and after some time it may rot. Therefore, it is very important to treat wood properly in areas with a higher level of humidity or frequent rains. Another disadvantage of wood is that it catches fire easily (that is, wood is a flammable material) but certain wood types can retain their strength for a long time without collapsing, when exposed to fire.

Plastic is a synthetic material, a compound made of petrochemicals whose features very strongly depend on the different components. Cheap plastic is usually a light but brittle material, meanwhile high-quality, expensive plastic is not only light, but also fairly strong in compression and tension. High-quality plastic is normally either ductile or elastic (depending on its components) due to its long chains of molecules. Another advantage is that it is moldable to different shapes. A disadvantage of plastic is that some of its components may release toxic fumes when it is exposed to fire and therefore plastic can be a health hazard. In general, most plastic used in constructions (and also in everyday life) is not biodegradable and therefore the use of this material causes severe problems for the environment. Biodegradable plastic doesn't pose such risks to the environment, but unfortunately its production is still quite expensive.

Task 1:   Are the following sentences true or false? Correct the false sentences based on <u>what you read</u>.

1.   The tensile strength of concrete can be improved by adding steel or fiberglass to it.

2.   Wood is highly flammable, so wooden structures always burn down very fast.

3.   Plastic is basically a light and elastic material.

4.   Plastic is an alloy.

5.   A disadvantage of brick is that it sometimes releases toxic fumes when it burns.

6.   Aluminum alloy is lightweight, strong in tension and compression, but also expensive.

7.   Steel has a higher amount of carbon than cast iron.

8.   Concrete and cast iron are equally brittle and they both break without any initial cracks.

9.   Wood is the only biodegradable construction material.

10. Wood can rot when it is exposed to too much water.

Task 2: Which of the three materials would you use for the following parts of a building construction? Explain why you would choose that material.

When explaining your choice, use
- the expressions: "too ...." and "not ... enough"
- comparisons "not as ... as", "more ... than...", the most ..."

1. the foundation of a garden shed:　　　　1. reinforced concrete　　2. concrete　　3. gravel

   Reason:

2. the foundation of a skyscraper:　　　　1. reinforced concrete　　2. concrete　　3. brick

   Reason:

3. the walls of a two-storey family home:　　　　1. brick　　2. concrete　　3. wood

   Reason:

4. the roof of a sports arena　　　1. corrugated sheets　　2. plastic　　3. ceramic tiles

   Reason:

5. the railings of the stairway in a block of flats:　　1. cast iron　　2. steel　　3. stainless steel

   Reason:

6. the faucets / taps in a bathroom:　　　　1. cast iron　　2. aluminum　　3. stainless steel

   Reason:

7. the electric roller shutters of a garage door　　　1. wood　　2. aluminum　　3. plastic

   Reason:

Preparing presentations in a technical area

Giving a presentation always requires thorough preparations and enough practice. Beyond that, engineers in an international environment face some additional challenge as they are often confronted with the task of having to give a presentation in a job-related, technical area speaking fluent English. Here are some useful pieces of advice to facilitate the preparation.

1. To start with, make sure you are **well informed** on the topic you are going to talk about. Select your materials carefully and read them thoroughly. Be sure to check the meanings of words you are not familiar with or you are uncertain about, using a reliable dictionary.

2. Adapt the language you use to your target audience to suit their needs and their level of competence. Keep in mind: non-native speakers of English may have difficulties understanding long and complex sentences or sophisticated words. Therefore, use simple sentences and clear, transparent sentence structures. Remember the KISS principle: **K**eep **I**t **S**hort and **S**imple!

3. You may want to prepare a **glossary** with some technical terms and expressions for your audience. Alternatively, you may explain unknown words / expressions in English during your presentation if time allows. Follow a simple principle: If you, a non-native speaker of English did not understand certain technical terms while preparing your presentation, your audience may not understand those terms in your talk, either. If they don't understand key vocabulary, they won't be able to follow you.

4. Prepare **cue cards** with the main points you wish to make. Cue cards will help you stay on track, remember key issues and use proper terms during your talk.

5. Keep track of time. Presenters are often given a time frame for the presentation. It is advisable to **time yourself** prior to the talk. Most people speak more slowly and need more time for arranging their thoughts when speaking in a foreign language. But some people tend to talk faster than usual when they are nervous. Test yourself before presenting in front of an audience.

6. When you prepare your slides, make sure they are

   - **legible** (make sure that people sitting in the back of the room are able to read it)
   - **relevant** (they are related to what you are talking about just when you are talking about it)
   - **concise** (avoid long sentences as you want the audience to listen to you attentively)
   - **attractive** (pictures/graphics spark the interest and help the audience visualize your ideas)
   - **accurate** (make sure you don't have typos on your slides)

7. Last but not least, don't forget to use **signposting** expressions in your presentation. With the help of linking words, you guide your audience through your talk: you connect your ideas to create logical sequences, refer to slides, refer back to previous information (that your audience should recall at a certain point), highlight particularly important concepts, compare and contrast ideas, express your own opinion, etc. Signposting makes your presentation dynamic, easy to follow and professional sounding.

Grammar task 1:   Read the following sentences that give you some advice on how to make a good presentation. Write the appropriate adjective or adverb (on the right) into the sentence (on the left).

Try to present your topic in   …………………………………….. English.   fluent / fluently
Select relevant details ………………………………………………….   careful / carefully
Be ……………………………. -informed about the topic in general.   good / well
During your talk, pay attention to …..…………..…………….. articulation.   clear / clearly
In other words, try to pronounce each word ………………………………..   clear / clearly
Keep your explanations short and ………………………………………….   simple / simply
Remember that you should speak ……………………………………………   free / freely
If you read out your text, it will ……………………………… reduce the   strong / strongly
value of your presentation.
Of course, you may ……………………………… look at your cue cards.   occasional/occasionally
It is better to speak a bit more …………………………….. than too fast.   slow / slowly
Then your audience will understand you more ………………………….   easy / easily
Use ……………………………. signposting language during your talk.   proper / properly
In your talk, highlight ……………………. important ideas using linking words.   particular/particularly
Also, it is ……………………………. to keep eye contact with your audience.   essential / essentially
Don't forget to have a ………..…………. summary at the end of your talk.   brief / briefly

Grammar task 2: Fill the following gaps with the appropriate adverbs from the box below.

unfortunately	eventually	hardly	recently
basically	obviously	actually	naturally

I heard a great presentation about the Shard in London ………………………………… (It was a few days ago.)

…………………………………………………., the presenter really liked this topic. (I was convinced about it.)

……………………………., it was about the new technologies used during the construction of the skyscraper.

……………………………….., we were busy taking notes while he was speaking. (Of course, we were!)

………………………………………………… he only had 30 minutes for his presentation. (What a pity!)

He …………………………………….. had any time to answer our questions when he finished his talk.

……………………………………………… he gave us his email address so we can contact him if we have some
more questions. (He did it at the end of his talk.)

…………………………………., I might indeed write him an email and ask him about some more details.

TOPIC 3
Tall buildings

This topic focuses on:

◊   Technologies used in skyscraper construction

◊   Challenges of building tall

◊   Describing buildings:

- Shapes

- Dimensions

◊   Grammar:

- If clauses

- Use of numbers

Technologies used in skyscraper construction

The emergence of skyscrapers in the United States at the end of the 19th century was enabled by economic growth and technological development. The ever-increasing need for useable space in the business districts of big cities with rapidly growing population (like Chicago or New York) led to the construction of more and more buildings that rose vertically instead of spreading horizontally.

The traditional **masonry walls** were not suitable for the construction of high-rise buildings: the solid brick or concrete walls would have needed to be very thick to ensure structural stability. But the massive thick walls would have increased the dead load way too much. The foundation would not have been strong enough to carry the largely increased weight and the building could have collapsed. Therefore, new technologies were necessary to be able to reach greater heights.

The very first tall buildings still used thick masonry walls at the ground levels, but the upper floors rested on a **steel framework** made of horizontal beams and vertical columns, which greatly reduced the dead load of the building.

The first skyscrapers built in the late-19th and early-20th centuries were moderately tall buildings. The ten-storey Chicago Home Insurance Building is considered to be the first modern skyscraper with a load-bearing **steel-girder framework**. It weighs only one third of what it would weigh if it had traditional stone masonry walls. Attached to the steel framework is a curtain wall: an outer covering made of lightweight materials (most of all glass) that only bears its own weight.

The construction of the first skyscrapers wouldn't have been possible without some ground-breaking technological inventions in construction and materials engineering. Henry Bessemer (1813 – 1898) became famous for drastically lowering the costs of manufacturing steel. The **Bessemer process** (a decarbonization process using a blast of air) is still in use in modern construction. It has made the mass production of steel possible, thus enabling steel to become the main structural component of tall buildings and allowing skyscrapers to reach greater heights.

Meanwhile the Bessemer process provided affordable material for skyscraper construction, George A. Fuller's (1851-1900) innovation offered the necessary technology for increasing the height of the buildings. Fuller tried to solve the potential challenge of insufficient load bearing capacities in tall buildings. In earlier constructions, the heavy and massive masonry walls carried the weight of the structure. Fuller, however, realized that he could use Bessemer steel for **horizontal beams** and **vertical columns** to give the building an **internal load-bearing structural framework** which was clad by **external, non-structural curtain walls**.

The curtain walls supported and surrounded the load-bearing skeleton, offered protection against wind load, provided a lot of natural light and gave buildings a modern flair. Besides the Chicago Home Insurance Building, further well-known first instances of using the steel framework construction technology are the Tacoma Building (Chicago, 1889) and the Flatiron Building (New York, 1902).

Despite all the advantages, this simple and effective construction method also had one significant drawback: as the height increased, the weight also increased and more supporting columns were necessary to bear the larger dead load. More columns meant less **useable floor space** because the additional supporting columns took up valuable space. In addition, the added columns further increased the weight of the structure. Therefore, steel frame constructions were no longer a reasonable and profitable option beyond a certain height.

In the early 1960s, a structural engineer, Fazlur Khan, began to develop a new support system for the construction of lighter, taller skyscrapers. His central innovation was the **tube structural system** where the building is designed like a hollow cylinder. It allows more economic efficiency and also a variety of different shapes. The tube structure requires less material and therefore cuts costs meanwhile it allows buildings to reach greater heights.

The **tube within a tube** architecture consists of a massive core in the center made of either reinforced concrete or a dense bundle of steel columns surrounded by closely-spaced external columns which form the building's **perimeter walls**.

The massive central core of the tube-framed skyscrapers holds the elevator shaft along with staircases and utility rooms. This inner tube provides basic structural stability. The outer tube (which consists of the perimeter walls) carries the majority of the lateral wind loads. Furthermore, much of the vertical gravity loads are also transferred to these perimeter walls.

The tube structural systems are fundamental to modern skyscraper design. Most buildings over 40-stories constructed since the 1960s use a tube design derived from Khan's structural engineering principles. One of the early examples of the tube construction were the Twin Towers in New York. Further examples of modern skyscrapers with tube construction include the Petronas Towers in Kuala Lumpur, the Shard in London and the Burj Khalifa in Dubai.

Comprehension task:

Are the following sentences true, false, or not mentioned in the text? If they are false, change the sentences and make correct statements.

1. The Chicago Home Insurance Building is an example of a construction with a steel structural framework.

   TRUE   FALSE   NOT MENTIONED

2. The modern structure of the building allowed the weight to be reduced by one third.

   TRUE   FALSE   NOT MENTIONED

3. Thanks to the Bessemer process, the production of steel became cheaper and the quality higher.

   TRUE   FALSE   NOT MENTIONED

4. The curtain walls of a skyscraper do not bear structural load.

   TRUE   FALSE   NOT MENTIONED

5. Fuller's innovation made it possible to build higher while greatly reducing the dead load.

   TRUE   FALSE   NOT MENTIONED

6. The greater the weight of a skyscraper, the more columns are necessary for structural support.

   TRUE   FALSE   NOT MENTIONED

7. The tube system makes it possible to build higher, but the construction is also more expensive.

   TRUE   FALSE   NOT MENTIONED

8. The tube system consists of a central core and perimeter walls surrounding the core.

   TRUE   FALSE   NOT MENTIONED

9. The inner "tube" carries all the vertical loads, while the outer tube carries all the horizontal loads.

   TRUE   FALSE   NOT MENTIONED

10. An advantage of the tube system is that it allows constructions to take on various different shapes.

    TRUE   FALSE   NOT MENTIONED

Shapes and dimensions

Vocabulary: 2D & 3D shapes

2D Shapes		3D Shapes	
nouns	adjectives	nouns	adjectives
triangle	triangular	pyramid	pyramidal
rectangle	rectangular	cube	cuboid
square	square	box	box-shaped
circle	circular	sphere	spherical
trapeze	trapezoid	cylinder	cylindrical
arch	arched	ellipse / oval	elliptical / oval
line	linear	cone	conical

Task: Describe the <u>shapes</u> and their <u>dimensions</u> below in full sentences. Describe as many details as you can (e.g. width, length, height, radius, ground surface area, volume).

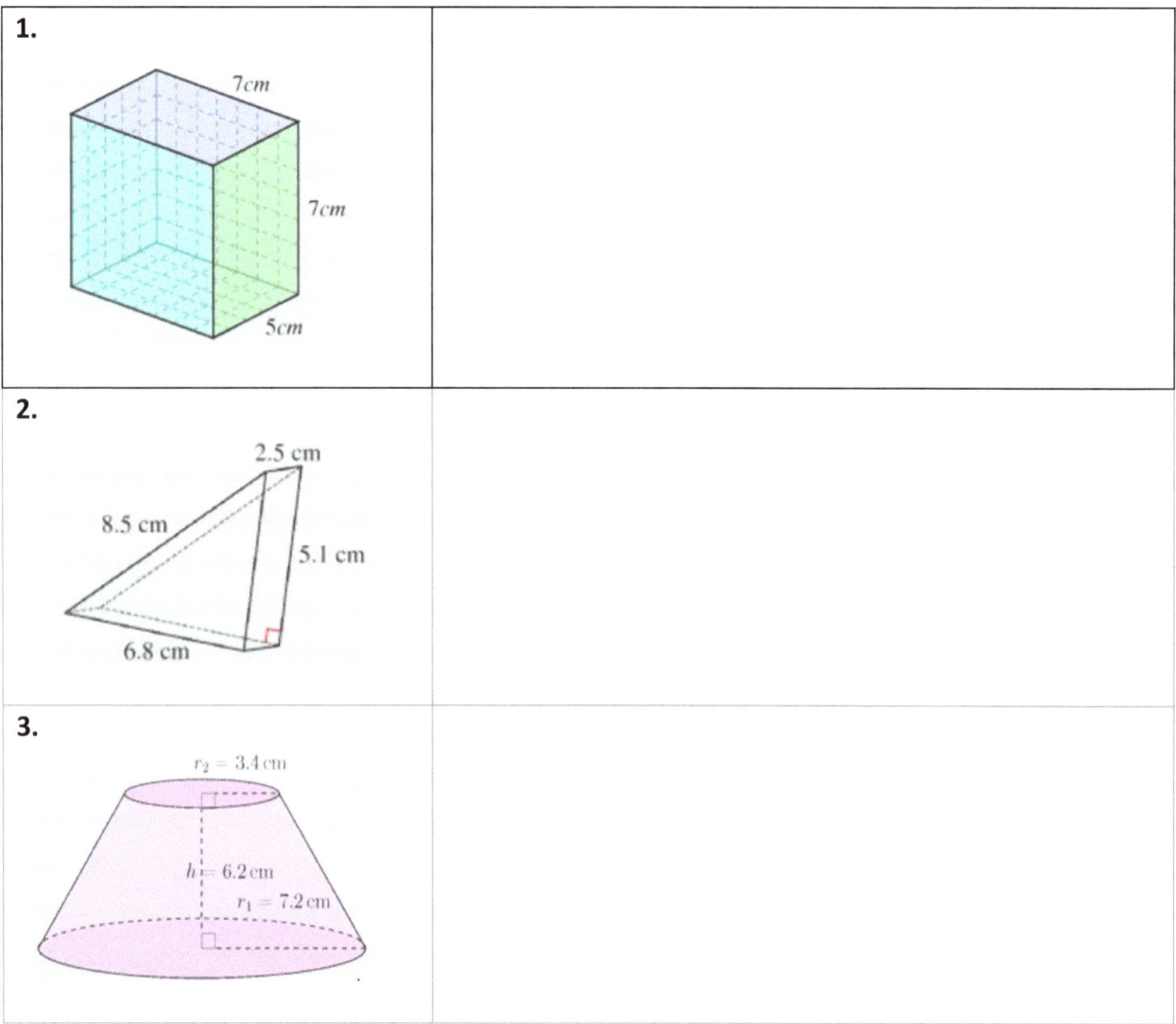

1.	
7cm 7cm 5cm	
2.	
2.5 cm 8.5 cm 5.1 cm 6.8 cm	
3.	
$r_2 = 3.4$ cm $h = 6.2$ cm $r_1 = 7.2$ cm	

The challenges of building tall

Loading challenges
A skyscraper experiences tremendous load from the building material itself. In technical terms, the **dead load** is larger than the **live load** (the weight of all the people/things in the structure).

The wind loading on a skyscraper is also considerable. In fact, the lateral wind load on super-tall structures is generally the governing factor in the structural design. Wind pressure increases with height, so for very tall buildings, the loads associated with wind are larger than dead or live loads.

Other vertical and horizontal loading factors come from varied, unpredictable sources, such as earthquakes.

Other challenges
Tall buildings must be accessible (by lift or stairways), even on the upper floors, and provide utilities (lighting, water, communications systems etc.) and a comfortable climate for the occupants (through air conditioning, heating, lighting etc.). There must also be comprehensive fire prevention and fire protection facilities in place and the building must be multi-functional so that all available space is rented out.

The construction of a tall building also poses severe practical problems such as how to lift workers, equipment and materials hundreds of metres in order to construct the upper floors. During the construction of the Shard in London or the Burj Khalifa in Dubai, for example, concrete had to be pumped several hundred metres vertically to complete the summit of the building.

Task: Make a list of the challenges faced by designers and builders of tall buildings based on what you read in the text.

1. ....

2. ....

3. ....

4. ....

5. ....

6. ....

7. ....

8. ....

9. ....

10. ....

Vocabulary task: Internet research

The following expressions are related to the construction of tall buildings. Find out what they mean and what their purpose is in building construction with the help of reliable internet resources. Summarize your findings in short.

1. base isolation

2. tuned mass damper

3. wind tunnel

Writing task: Hypothetical structural considerations

Look at the picture below and answer the following questions in a continuous text.

- Would it be possible to increase the height of such a triangle-shaped building?

- Would there be a height limit, in your opinion?

- What structural alterations would be necessary to consider?

- What challenges should be expected during construction if we made such a construction higher?

TOPIC 4
Bridges

This topic focuses on:

◊ Basic bridge designs

◊ The collapse of the Tacoma Narrows Bridge

◊ Writing tasks: describing and designing bridges

Basic Bridge Design

Pre-reading task: Match the words with the explanations. Write the letters to the numbers.

1. ___   2. ___   3. ___   4. ___   5. ___   6. ___   7. ___   8. ___

9. ___   10. ___   11. ___   12. ___   13. ___   14. ___   15. ___

1.	pier	a.	a horizontal structural component *(= beam)* that protrudes / projects in one direction and is supported at only one end
2.	pylon	b.	a type of abutment the cables of a suspension bridge are firmly attached to on both ends
3.	deck	c.	a solid beam under the deck that stiffens the deck and therefore increases the load bearing capacity and prevents potential buckling
4.	abutment	d.	the component at both ends of the bridge that transfers the loads from the superstructure into the substructure
5.	anchorage	e.	to allow loads to spread out evenly over a certain area, to distribute loads evenly
6.	cantilever	f.	concrete that contains steel rods which are stretched beforehand in order to become more resistant under tension when exposed to loads
7.	truss girder	g.	to bend, to give way under pressure or strain *(= tension)*
8.	plate girder	h.	to move loads from one area to another area
9.	pre-stressed concrete	i.	an open cross-bracing system (a kind of latticework) that stiffens the deck and therefore increases the load bearing capacity and prevents potential buckling
10.	oscillation	j.	a vertical structural component under the deck of a bridge that provides support against bending motion
11.	to span	k.	a tower-like structural component under and above the deck (in other words: a mast)
12.	to buckle	l.	to break suddenly and completely, often with a sharp sound
13.	to snap	m.	the horizontal beam that serves as the roadway of a bridge
14.	to dissipate loads	n.	to extend / to cover a distance from one end to the other end
15.	to transfer loads	o.	a periodic vibration, resonance

"We've come a long way since the Romans figured out how to cross a wide river using timber"

(The evolution of bridges, www.ice.org.uk)

Bridges are a vital part of our infrastructure, providing passage over various different types of obstacles, be it a valley, a river, a bay, a channel, a road or a railway track underneath.

Beam bridge

The simplest of all types of bridges is the beam bridge. It comprises of a horizontal beam, which could be a wooden log at its simplest. The weight of the beam and the live load (cross-over traffic) push straight down on the horizontal surface. The top surface of the beam is compressed, meanwhile the bottom of the beam is subjected to tension. If there is too much vertical load on the bridge, the beam may start to buckle and eventually break.

A continuous-span beam bridge

To counteract the potential bending, beam bridges are normally supported by **piers** under the **deck**, one at both ends of the bridge. The closest the piers, the more structural stability they provide.

Besides the supporting piers under the **roadway**, beam bridges also need **abutments** on both ends. The abutments prevent horizontal motions of the deck that could cause shearing stress and they transfer loads from the superstructure to the substructure. Beam bridges cannot normally span more than 80 meters. This, however, doesn't mean that a beam bridge cannot provide passage for a greater distance. Short-span beam bridges can easily be connected to each other to create a so-called **continuous span**. Such beam bridges are supported by several piers underneath.

Truss bridge

It is possible to extend the span of a beam bridge by strengthening it with a cross bracing system, the so-called **truss**, that is made up of diagonal and vertical members, forming an assembly of interconnected triangles.

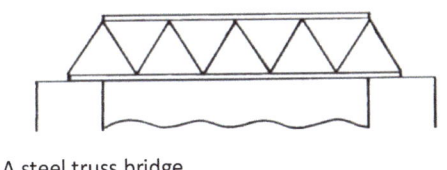

A steel truss bridge

The truss greatly increases the rigidity of the beam and helps dissipate the compression and tension. Therefore, truss bridges can span a longer distance than beam bridges and they can form a continuous span – up to 400 meters – without additional supporting piers.

Nevertheless, the longer the bridge, the bigger and sturdier the supporting truss must be. At a certain length, the truss cannot support the bridge's own weight any more.

Arch bridge

Another way to support the deck of a bridge is with the help of an arch. The arch bridge has great natural strength due to its semicircular shape.

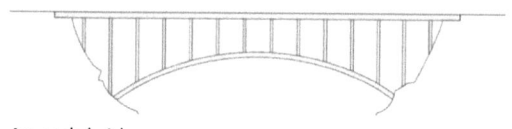

An arch bridge

The top surface of the arch is under tension, meanwhile the bottom is under compression. The loads are carried along the curve into the abutments that transfer the loads into the substructure.

The solid abutments at both ends of the arch push back against the structure, preventing the arch from spreading apart. Since the top surface of the arch is under tension, it prevents buckling when the beam is exposed to a lot of live load. The ancient stone arch bridges could only span a short distance due to their high dead load. Today's modern steel arches can span more than 500 meters.

Cantilever bridge

In 1867, engineer Heinrich Gerber designed a unique combination of the truss bridge and the arch bridge: the "Hassfurt Mainbrücke", which was the first **cantilever bridge**. Listed among the most modern constructions of that time, the Hassfurt bridge had a main span of merely 38 m. Today's cantilever bridges can span more than 500 m.

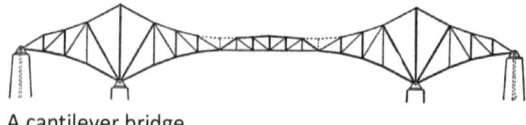

A cantilever bridge

This type of bridge consists of two rigid arms, the so-called **cantilever arms**, made up of diagonal steel braces.

They project horizontally into space and are attached to a pier at only one end. The two cantilever arms aren't connected to each other in the center. Instead, they are connected to the **central span** of the bridge – also a truss structure – which rests on the cantilever arms on both sides. The arms lift the central span and hold it in place. To enable this, the bridge must have solid anchorages on both ends. The so-called **anchor arms** on both sides connect the **piers** to the **anchorages**. The tensile force is transferred from the anchor arms into the solid anchor blocks.

Suspension bridge

With its main span lifted up and held under tension by the outstretched arms, the cantilever bridge in fact conforms to the main principle of a suspension bridge. The concept of a suspension bridge goes back to thousands of years in history, "...back to the days when our arboreal ancestors formed living chains of their own bodies, holding to each other with arms, legs, and tails, thus constructing suspension bridges across the water from the overhanging branches of opposite trees, in order to let their tribe pass over in safety to the other side." (John Alexander Low Waddell 1854–1938).

A suspension bridge

The man-made suspension bridges of modern times are composed of a deck that is suspended by massive **steel cables** draped over two towers and secured into solid

concrete blocks (the **anchorages**) on both ends of the bridge. These anchorages act as counterweights and keep the cables constantly under tension. The main cables consist of **strands of wires,** with wires about as thick as pencils. Thousands of these wires are draped over the two towers back and forth. They are passed over the **cable saddles** on top of the towers, bundled into strands and attached to the so-called "eye-bars" that are cemented into the solid anchorages. This process of making the bridge cables is called **cable spinning**. The main cables are connected to the roadway by steel ropes called **suspenders**. They provide additional support for the main cables holding the deck in place.

When vehicles push down on the roadway, the main cables transfer the loads from the **suspended deck** into the two **towers** and from there by vertical compression down to the substructure. Since the towers carry the weight of the cables and transfer the forces into the substructure, the suspension bridges need massive foundations firmly built on **bedrock**. The anchorages must be able to resist the strong pull of the cables and the two towers must be able to support most of the bridge's weight. Suspension bridges can have a very large span of up to almost 2000 meters. The 4 km-long Akashi Kaikyo bridge in Japan has a main span of 1991 m and it is currently the bridge with the longest span in the world.

Cable-stayed bridge

The most modern bridge type with a suspended deck is the cable-stayed bridge. Yet, the cable-stayed bridge supports the deck with steel cables in a different way.

A cable-stayed bridge

There are several cables (the so-called **stays**) attached to the roadway that run directly from the roadway up to a **tower** (also called **pylon**), forming a unique "A" shape. The cables are attached to the roadway and to the tower as well.

Other than that, they lift the **deck** based on the same principle as the suspension bridge: the strained cables hold the deck in place and the towers transfer the forces to the substructure through vertical compression. Cable-stayed bridges are the most popular alternatives for medium-length spans (between 152m and 915m).

Task 1: Answer the following questions based on what you read.

1) Why do beam bridges need piers under the deck?

2) What is the difference between an abutment and an anchorage?

3) What is the difference between a pier and a pylon?

4) What do cantilever, suspension and cable-stayed bridges have in common?

5) How is the central span of a cantilever bridge held in place?

6) Why does the arch shape have a great natural strength?

7) Why can't an arch bridge made of stone cover a long span?

8) What is a truss and how can it increase the stability of the beam bridge?

9) How do the cables of a suspension bridge and a cable-stayed bridge differ?

10) Why does the suspension bridge need solid anchorages and firm tower foundations?

Task 2: Express your opinion when answering the following questions.

1) Which bridge do you think takes the longest to construct? Why?

2) Which bridge is the most suitable for viaducts? Why?

3) Why is the truss design so often chosen for railway bridges?

4) Why is it so important to protect the steel cables of suspension bridges against corrosion?

5) Which bridge type is most suitable in areas with an earthquake hazard? Why?

Task 3: Describe a bridge

Prepare a short description of the Astoria Megler Bridge connecting the state of Washington with Oregon. In the table below, you will find all the details you need (construction information and measurements). Read the data carefully and write a **continuous text**, based on the given details. Make your text **attractive**! Write full sentences, connect pieces of information using linking words, highlight interesting / surprising facts. Write **10 - 15 sentences**.

Example based on the construction data of the New River Gorge Bridge:

The New River Gorge Bridge
Type: arch bridge / viaduct
Location: Fayetteville, West Virginia (US)
Total length: 924 m
Main span: 518 m
Height: 267 m
Completion date: 22. October, 1977

The New River Gorge Bridge is a magnificent viaduct stretching over a valley at Fayetteville in West Virginia. The bridge has a 924 m long roadway supported by a steel arch underneath. It emerges 267 m above the valley. With a main span of 518 m, this was the longest arch bridge in the world when it was completed in October 1977, and it belongs to the arch bridges with the longest main spans ever since.

Now describe the Astoria-Megler Bridge in a continuous text, similar to the given example above.

Name: Astoria-Megler Bridge
Design: continuous-span cantilever through-truss
Locale: Astoria (Oregon), Megler (WA)
Crosses: Columbia River
Carries: 2 vehicle lanes, 2 bicycle paths
Total length: 6545 m
Width: 8.5 m
Number of spans: 3 (main), 33 (approach)
Central span: 376 m

Clearance below: 60 m (high tide)
Piers in water: 171
Wind resistance: max 240 km/h
Construction cost: $24 million
Construction start: 5. November 1962
Completion date: 27. August, 1966
Opened: 29. July, 1966
Daily traffic: 7100
Toll: none (since 1993)

Task 4: Design a bridge

Imagine you are a structural engineer who has been commissioned to design a bridge in one of the following locations. Consider the four different options, then choose **one location** and write a continuous text, based on the following questions:

- What aspects of the <u>location</u> would you need to take into consideration for your design plan?
- After considering those aspects, what <u>type</u> of bridge would you choose?
- What <u>materials</u> would you use for the <u>different parts</u> of your bridge?
- What would be the <u>advantages</u> of your bridge type and the chosen materials?
- Can you think of any <u>problems, challenges</u> you would face during the construction of the bridge?

You are welcome to draw a sketch of your bridge in the chosen location, too.

Location 1: A 2 km long loop (= circular walkway) across a wetland park in Louisiana, US

Location 2: A bridge over a river that is approximately 450 m wide and connects two historic villages in a natural setting

Location 3: A skybridge that connects two twin skyscrapers on the 30th floor in order to provide passage between the upper levels of the two buildings

Location 4: A bridge that connects a small island that is approx. 900 m away from the mainland, in an area with strong winds and earthquake hazard

The collapse of the Tacoma Narrows Bridge

Pre-watching task 1: Explain these words / find synonyms with the help of a dictionary, if necessary.

come crashing down ....

slender ....

extraordinary ....

to bounce ....

hydraulic jacks ....

wind deflection devices ....

faulty engineering ....

wind eddies ....

amplitude ....

mandatory ....

dependable ....

Pre-watching task 2: Fill the gaps using some of the words / expressions <u>from the previous task</u>

The bridge collapsed because of ....

Long-lasting bridges are strong and ....

It is .... to check the structural stability of planned constructions.

If .... or .... are in-
stalled on a bridge, the natural oscillation can be reduced greatly.

When a bridge moves rhythmically up and down, it ....

**Now watch the documentary about the collapse of the Tacoma Narrows bridge (link to documentary:
<u>https://www.youtube.com/watch?v=KqqyAZDpV6c</u>) and answer the following questions.**

1. What type of a bridge is the Tacoma Narrows bridge?

....

2. How long was the bridge <u>in use</u> before it collapsed?

....

3. What were the two really extraordinary features of this bridge?

a. ....

b. ....

4. The famous bridge engineer, Leon Moisseiff was responsible for the final design plans of the bridge. He suggested an important <u>change</u> on the original design. What was this change?

5. Why did this change become a major cause of the collapse? Explain it in your own words.

6. Did the wind play a role in the collapse of the bridge? If yes, why?

7. Describe the collapse of the bridge. What part of the bridge came crashing down first? What happened next?

8. Were there any casualties?

9. Bridge engineering learned a lot from the collapse of the Tacoma Narrows bridge, engineers set some new standards for future suspension bridges. What are the <u>two most important changes</u> that were introduced in the design and construction of bridges after the disaster?

10. To sum up, describe the main differences in the <u>appearance</u> of the old Tacoma bridge (Galloping Gertie) and the new Tacoma bridge (Sturdy Gertie) that clearly show the changes in the structural design that were introduced after the collapse.

Supplementary Grammar:

- ## Grammar rules

- ## Examples

- ## Exercises

Modal verbs / auxiliaries

Underline the <u>most appropriate</u> modal verb in the following sentences.

1. There are plenty of tomatoes in the fridge. You *may / needn't / mustn't* buy any.

2. You *don't have to / mustn't / needn't* smoke in the laboratory.

3. He has been working for about 11 hours. He *must / can't / needs to* be tired after such hard work.

4. The teacher says we *must / may / can't* read this book for our own pleasure as it is optional.

5. Tim's flight from Sydney took more than 23 hours. He *can / need / must* be exhausted now.

6. If you want to speak English fluently, you *have to / need / may* practice much.

7. People *needn't / mustn't / don't have to* walk on the grass. There's a sign: "Keep off the grass".

8. Drivers *may / need / must* stop when the traffic lights are red.

9. *Need / May / Must* I ask a question? Yes, of course. Go ahead!

10. You *mustn't / needn't / doesn't need to* take your umbrella. It is not raining.

11. *May / Need / Can* you speak Italian? No, I'm afraid I *may not / needn't / can't*.

12. You really *shouldn't / don't need to / can* cross the road here. There's no zebra crossing and there's heavy traffic. You *should / mustn't / can't* go across the street at the traffic lights.

13. We are finished for today. You *don't have to / needn't / may* leave now.

14. Susan *can't / won't / couldn't* hear the speaker because there was a lot of background noise.

15. The subcontractor *mustn't / doesn't have to / needn't* postpone the delivery because the materials are needed on the construction site immediately.

16. You *mustn't / don't have to / shouldn't* be rich to be a success. Some of the most successful artists are very famous without being wealthy.

17. There *may / can / must* be something we can do! We *needn't / may not / mustn't* just give up without even trying!

18. The earthquake caused major damage to the building, so the residents *mustn't / can't / weren't allowed to* return to their homes. They were brought to a temporary camp.

19. If I learn some Spanish, I *can / will be able to / mustn't* order my meal in Spanish in Mallorca.

20. It was not possible to renovate the old house. It *must / had to / will have to* be demolished last year.

The passive voice

How to form the passive:

The object of the active sentence becomes the subject of the passive sentence. It is followed by "be" (in the appropriate tense) + the third form of the verb.

He writes **a letter**   →   **The letter** is written **by him.**

The use of the passive in the most common tenses:

	Active	Passive
Simple Present	Structural engineers often carry out feasibility studies.	Feasibility **studies are often carried out** by structural engineers.
Present Continuous	They **are painting** the walls now.	The walls **are being painted** now.
Simple Past	The storm **tore off some roof shingles.**	Some roof shingles **were torn off** by the storm.
Past Continuous	They **were pouring concrete** this time last week.	**Concrete was being poured** this time last week.
Present Perfect	Some engineering students **have visited** the construction site.	The construction site **has been visited** by some engineering students.
Simple Future *will*	They **will finish work on** the foundation by next Monday.	Work on the foundation **will be finished** by next Monday
Modal verbs (e.g. must)	The workers **must wear** helmets.	Helmets **must be worn** by the workers.

The passive voice - exercise

Put the following sentences into passive.

1. Someone stole my car!

....

2. The gardener cuts off some old branches.

....

3. Talented journalists write interesting articles.

....

4. They will build a new book store near the railway station.

....

5. The workers bring heavy machines to the site.

....

6. You shouldn't leave the door open!

....

7. They pay the agent 5 % commission after each successful purchase.

....

8. They put off the meeting because the chairman got ill.

....

9. The construction manager must oversee the entire construction project.

....

10. The structural engineer is going to draw the first design plan in the coming days.

....

Comparisons

Comparative is the name for the grammar used <u>when comparing two things</u>. The two basic ways to compare are using **as .. as**, when two things have the same features or <u>... **than,**</u> when two things show differences in a certain feature. When two things show differences in a certain feature, we can also use **not as ... as**.

Examples:

- A family home in the countryside is not **as** expensive **as** an apartment in the city center.
- The supermarket is just **as** far from my home **as** the university campus.
- Today, the cafeteria is not **as** crowded **as** usual.
- Our European clients are not as difficult to negotiate with **as** our Asian clients.
- Our company built twice **as** many houses **as** any other construction companies in the area.

- A family home in the countryside is cheaper **than** an apartment in the city center.
- The supermarket is not **farther / further** away from my home **than** the university campus.
- Today, the cafeteria is **emptier than** usual.
- The Asian clients are **more difficult** to negotiate with **than** the European clients.
- Our company built much **more** houses **than** any other construction companies in the area.

When comparing with **as .. as**, the adjective does not change. When comparing with **than**, however, some changes are necessary, depending on the number of syllables the adjective has:

<u>1-syllable adjectives</u>**:** add **-er** to the adjective

- A skyscraper is much **taller** than a bungalow.
- Plastic is **lighter** than iron.
- Reinforced concrete is **stronger** in tension than cast iron.

Note: If the word has a *consonant-vowel-consonant sequence*, then the last consonant is usually doubled in the comparative. Examples: *big-bigger, fat-fatter, hot-hotter*.

<u>2-syllable adjectives ending in -y</u>: change the **-y** to **-ier**

- Reinforced concrete is **heavier** than brick.
- Cast iron is **easier** to mould to shape than cement.

Attention! Do not confuse adjectives and adverbs. 2-syllable <u>adverbs</u> ending in **-ly** must be compared with the word *"more"*. Example: *Aluminum deforms **more quickly** than iron.*

<u>Other 1-syllable and 2-syllable adjectives</u>: in most cases use **more** with the unchanged adjective

- Cast iron is **more brittle** than steel.
- The neighborhood we live in is economically **more stable** than the one we used to live in.
- Tokyo is **more crowded** than London.

Adjectives with 3 or more syllables: <u>Always</u> use **more** with the unchanged adjective

- French is **more difficult** to learn than English.
- A construction manager's job is **more interesting** than the job of a bank clerk.

The superlative form

In the *superlative* you talk about <u>one thing only</u> and how it is the best, worst, etc. You <u>do not</u> compare *two* things. The following guidelines apply to the superlative:

1-syllable adjectives: add **-est** to the adjective (plus *the*)

- Burj Khalifa is currently **the tallest** building in the world.
- The American subprime mortgage crisis was one of **the worst** real estate crises in recent history.
- Tokyo belongs to the cities with **the highest** population in the world.

Note: If the word has a *consonant-vowel-consonant sequence*, then the last consonant is usually doubled in the superlative. Examples: ***big-biggest, fat-fattest, hot-hottest***.

2-syllable adjectives ending in -y: change the **-y** to **-iest** (plus *the*)

- Cast iron belongs to the heaviest construction materials.
- Wood is an organic material and therefore **the easiest** to reproduce.

Attention! Do not confuse adjectives and adverbs. 2-syllable adverbs ending in **-ly** form their superlative with *"the most"*. Example: *Of all the people I know my father drives **<u>the most quickly.</u>***

Other 1-syllable and 2-syllable adjectives: use **the most** with the unchanged adjective

- **The most robust** buildings have reinforced concrete foundation.
- Cheap plastic belongs to **the most brittle** materials.

Adjectives with 3 or more syllables: use **the most** with the unchanged adjective

- Albert Einstein was one of the **most intelligent** scientists in history.
- You can usually find **the most expensive** buildings in city centers.

The most common <u>irregular</u> comparative & superlative forms:

good	better	the best
bad	worse	the worst
far	farther/further	farthest/furthest
much	more	most
little	less	least

Task: Compare the following materials. Use adjectives from the table below and follow the instructions.

light	brittle	durable	hard	cheap	flammable	(has) a smooth surface
heavy	elastic	weak	soft	expensive	mouldable	(has) a rough surface

1. _**Compare these materials using the basic form of comparison (as …. as / not as … as…)**_

bamboo and plywood

....

aluminum and stainless steel

....

slate and ceramic

....

2. _**Compare these materials using the comparative form (…-er than …. / more … than …)**_

cast iron and steel
....

timber and plastic ....

brick and veneer ....

3. _**Use the superlative form of an adjective (from the table) to describe these materials**_
   **(is the ….-est / is the most …)**

Reinforced concrete is ....

....

Plastic ....

....

Rubber is ....

....

The use of adjectives and adverbs

Adjective: they usually come **before nouns**

He gave us a _clear_ explanation.
He is quite a _quick_ painter.
This city has a _steady_ population growth.
He is a _bad_ construction manager.

Adverbs: they usually come **after action verbs**

He explained everything _clearly_.
He paints walls quite _quickly_.
The population of this city grows _steadily_.
He manages his workers _badly_.

Exception : good → well   I am a _good_ student. → I do _well_ at school.

List of irregular advebs (= no formal difference between adjective and adverb):

hard	hard
fast	fast
early	early
daily	daily

It is a _daily / weekly / monthly_ …journal.
I'm an _early_ bird.
He's a _fast_ driver.
My brother is a _hard_ worker.

It is published _daily / weekly / monthly_…
I usually get up _early_.
He drives _fast_.
He works _hard_.

FURTHER use of adverbs
Adverbs are also used to give extra information about adjectives (or other adverbs). They make the meaning of the adjectives / adverbs more concrete.

- They finished the substructure _surprisingly_ quickly.
- It is _particularly_ important to calculate the potential wind loads.
- The water level has risen _dangerously_ high during high tide.
- The excavation works took <u>unexpectedly</u> long.
- The construction costs were _considerably_ higher than expected.

EXCEPTIONS! We use **adjectives** with certain verbs, for example **seem, look, appear, sound**

- This building looks _old_.
- The tower seems (to be) _large_.
- The giant drills sound _horrible_.

Attention! Some adverbs refer to the WHOLE SENTENCE. They often start the sentence.

Basically, it is the structural engineer who considers the feasibility of a structural design.
Actually, the tallest skyscraper in the world is still the Burj Khalifa.
Eventually, the contractor managed to resolve the conflict between the client and the architect.

Prepositions

Grammar task : Underline the most suitable preposition in the following sentences.

1. The construction workers are working *into / on / in* the foundation at the moment.

2. The manager came *out / out of / at* his office and went *in / into / at* the kitchen to make tea.

3. He ran *across / inside / opposite* the road, ignoring the red light.

4. I sat *below / beside / between* the taxi driver, and my wife sat in *front of / across / behind* me.

5. The strong winds tore some shingles *off / out of / around* the roof.

6. We need a boat to get *up / over / out* the river which flows **into / through / around** the town.

7. They built a fence *above / down / around* their garden.

8. We cannot build a cellar because the soil is too soft *on / beneath / into* the ground.

9. I live *in / on / at* the 6th floor *in / on / at* 28 Tumbridge Road *in / on / at* Manchester.

10. The hotel restaurant is *beyond / beneath / between* the 19th and the 21st floors.

11. Is the drug store far away? No, it is right *towards / next to / into* the hospital over there.

12. There is only one skyscraper *above / along / among* these buildings here which was built more than 30 years ago.

13. I thought someone was standing *in front of / opposite / behind* me, but when I turned around, I didn't see anybody.

14. Geotechnical engineers spend a lot of time *behind / in front of / on* their computer screens.

15. We walked two miles *above / through / along* the river till we finally found the restaurant.

16. There's a helicopter hovering *over / up / out of* our house.

17. When the dog saw his owner, he started to run *towards / away / across* him.

18. The strong currents *above / under / around* the bridge risk the stability of the bridge.

19. Those beautiful mountains are *between / in / beyond* the country's borders.

If-clauses / Conditionals Type 1, 2 and 3

Overview with examples

Type 1	Type 2	Type 3
If he **goes** fast, he **will** catch the train.	If he **went** fast, he **would catch** the train.	If he **had gone** fast, he **would have caught** the train.
If he **doesn't stay out** at night, he **will get** enough sleep.	If he **didn't stay out** at night, he **would get** enough sleep.	If he **hadn't stayed out** at nights, he **would have gotten** enough sleep.
If they **are interested**, they **will call** us back.	If they **were interested**, they **would call** us back.	If they **had been interested**, they **would have called** us back.
If I **see** him, I **will tell** him to wait.	If I **saw** him, I **would tell** him to wait.	If I **had seen** him, I **would have told** him to wait.

Type 1 Conditional

It expresses **probability**. (Something will very likely happen.) It connects two future actions. One of these future actions must happen, to make the other possible /probable.

How to form:

The verb in the "if" clause is *in the present tense*. The verb in the main clause *follows "will"*

Instead of *"if"* we can also use *"in case"*.

- If I have time, I will help you.
- In case I have time, I will help you.

"if" clause: "If I have time," / "In case I have time,"

Main clause: "I will help you."

Meaning : It is possible that I have time (in the future). In that case, I will help you.

Type 2 Conditional

It expresses **unlikely** or **impossible situations** in the present.

How to form:

The verb in the "if" clause is *in the simple past tense*. The verb in the main clause *follows "would"*.

- If I had time, I would help you.

"if" clause: "If I had time,"   (Conditional 2 → but I do NOT have time)

Main clause: "I would help you."

Type 3 Conditional

It expresses that **something did not happen, because a certain condition was missing**. It always refers to the past.

How to form:

The verb in the "if" clause is in the past perfect tense (had + third form). The main clause is made up of "would have" + third form of the verb (also called: past participle)

- If I had found a good job, I would have earned much money.

"if" clause: "If I had found a good job," (Conditional 3 → But I DID NOT find a good job, …)

Main clause: "I would have earned much money." (…so I did not earn much money.)

Type 0 Conditional

It describes a so called "general truth", where one action /state leads automatically leads to another action / state. It is not really a conditional sentence (there is no "condition here).

How to form:

The verb in the "if" clause and the verb in the main clause are in the present tense. We can use "when" instead of "if".

- *If we wood catches fire, it burns.*

Meaning: Wood always burns when / if it catches fire. It is a general truth.

- If I have time, I help you.

Meaning : I always help you, whenever I have the time for that. It is generally true.

Task 1: What type conditional are these sentences? Write the type and translate the sentences.

1.   If the summit of the building reached 1 m higher, this skyscraper would be the tallest in the country.

Type: ……………………. Translation: ………………………………………………………………………..

……..

2.   If concrete is poured over a gridwork of steel bars, it gets much stronger in tension.

Type: ……………………. Translation: ………………………………………………………………………..

……..

3.   If we increase the height of this building by 10 meters, the dead load will exceed the maximum load bearing capacity.

Type: ……………………. Translation: ………………………………………………………………………

……..

4.   If the architect had consulted with the structural engineer in the planning phase, they wouldn't have had so many feasibility issues during construction.

Type: ……………………. Translation: ……………………………………………………………………..

……

Task 2: Re-write the sentences using proper conditionals. Your sentence must have the same meaning as the original sentence.

1.   This building can only resist a 7.5 magnitude earthquake.

If the earthquake ……………………………………………………………………………………………………..

2.   This city doesn't use ITS (Intelligent Transport System). No wonder there are so many traffic jams.

But if they ………..

3.   The dead load of this warehouse can't be increased without having settlement problems as a consequence.

If you ………

4.   This supermarket is built without an underground parking because the budget doesn't allow it.

But if the budget …………………………………………………………………………………………………….

5.   The dam broke and so the town got flooded.

But if the dam ……………………………………………………………………………………………………..

Task 3: Look at the notes below and make full sentences out of them, using Conditional Type I

Example: Soft soil under the construction → settlement problems

      *If the soil **is** soft / If **there is** soft soil under the building, there **will be** settlement problems.*

1.   structural calculations accurate → building structurally stable

If ....

2.   wood not treated properly → rot

If ....

3.   concrete reinforced with steel bars → much stronger in tension and compression

If ....

4.   finish foundation by Friday → start masonry on Monday

If ....

Task 4: Re-phrase the following sentences using Conditional Type II.

Example:

Steel rusts, so we need to protect the joints in the structure.

*If steel **didn't rust**, we **wouldn't need to** protect the joints in the structure.*

1.   Many old houses aren't adequately insulated, so the rooms heat up easily in the summer.

If ....

2.   Lifts and stairs can't be used in case of fire, so people are often stuck in a burning skyscraper.

If ....

3.   Modern skyscrapers don't have traditional masonry walls, so the dead load is much lower.

If ....

4.   People don't think of flood hazards and so they often build their houses right next to a river.

If ....

Sources, recommended further readings

Main areas of civil engineering

https://www.mcgill.ca/civil/undergrad/areas
http://engineering.iu.edu.sa/index.php/sub-disciplines-of-civil-engineering/
https://www.careeraddict.com/top-10-skills-needed-for-a-job-in-civil-engineering

Loads and forces

https://www.pbs.org/wgbh/buildingbig/lab/
https://www.designingbuildings.co.uk/wiki/Types_of_structural_load
https://theconstructor.org/structural-engg/types-of-loads-on-structure/1698/
https://scienceaid.net/Force_and_Stresses_in_Civil_Engineering

Building materials

https://theconstructor.org/building/types-of-building-materials-construction/699/
https://www.britannica.com/topic-browse/Technology/Materials/Building-Materials
http://www.technologystudent.com/joints/matprop1.htm
http://www.aboutcivilengineering.com/2018/04/05/engineering-properties-of-building-materials-and-their-importance/

Tall buildings

http://www.madehow.com/Volume-6/Skyscraper.html
https://www.thoughtco.com/how-skyscrapers-became-possible-1991649
https://science.howstuffworks.com/engineering/structural/skyscraper.htm
https://searchinginhistory.blogspot.com/2015/06/the-bessemer-process-process-that-made.html
https://constructible.trimble.com/construction-industry/the-building-technology-behind-a-mile-high-skyscraper

Bridges

https://www.britannica.com/technology/bridge-engineering
http://www.bridgesdb.com/bridge-history-facts/historical-development-of-bridges/
http://www.historyofbridges.com/facts-about-bridges/
https://www.designingbuildings.co.uk/wiki/Bridge_construction
https://www.brighthubengineering.com/structural-engineering/59793-bridge-design-planning-and-con-struction/
https://www.ice.org.uk/events/exhibitions/ice-bridge-engineering-exhibition/the-history-of-bridges

https://structurae.de/bauwerke/mainbruecke-hassfurt-1867
https://en.wikipedia.org/wiki/Astoria%E2%80%93Megler_Bridge
http://design-technology.org/
https://www.researchgate.net/publication/295258027_Brief_History_of_Suspension_Bridges

The Tacoma Narrows bridge

https://www.simscale.com/blog/2018/07/tacoma-narrows-bridge-collapse/
http://www.engineering.com/DesignerEdge/water/ArticleID/171/Tacoma-Bridge.aspx
Link to video: https://www.youtube.com/watch?v=KqqyAZDpV6c

Technical English Course materials

Markner-Jäger (2013) Technical English – Civil Engineering and Construction. Haan-Gruiten: Verlag Europa Lehrmittel

Ibbotson (2008) Cambridge English for Engineering. Cambridge University Press

Complete Glossary in Alphabetical Order

ability (n)	Fähigkeit	Topics 1,2
able (a)	fähig	Topic 1
abutment (n)	Balkenkopf, Stützmauer, Widerlager	Topic 4
accessible (a)	zugänglich	Topic 3
act on something (v)	auf etwas einwirken	Topic 2
actually (adv)	eigentlich, tatsächlich	Topic 2
add (v)	hinzufügen	Topic 2
adjust (v)	anpassen	Topic 3
advantage (n)	Vorteil	Topics 2, 3
advice (n)	Ratschlag	Topic 1
advise (v)	beraten	Topic 1
affordable (a)	kostengünstig, bezahlbar	Topic 3
alloy (n)	Legierung	Topic 1
along (prep)	entlang	Topic 4
among (prep)	unter ... (mehreren Sachen)	Topic 4
ancestors (n)	Vorfahren	Topic 4
anchor (v)	verankern	Topic 4
anchorage (n)	Verankerung	Topic 4
angle (n)	Winkel	Topic 3
appearance (n)	Aussehen	Topic 4
appliances (n)	Geräte	Topic 1
application (n)	Anwendung, Bewerbung	Topic 2
apply (v)	anwenden, auftragen	Topic 2
appropriate (a)	angemessen, passend	Topic 1
approximately (adv)	ungefähr	Topic 2
arboreal (a)	auf Bäumen lebend	Topic 4
arch (n)	Bogen	Topic 3
arched (a)	gebogen, bogenförmig	Topic 3
areal (a)	gebietlich, räumlich, regional	Topic 1
arise (v)	entstehen, auftauchen	Topic 1
arrange (v)	einrichten, vereinbaren	Topic 1
assembly (n)	Baugruppe, Verband	Topic 4
assess (v)	einschätzen, auswerten, bewerten	Topic 1
assessment (n)	Einschätzung, Bewertung, Gutachten	Topic 1
attach (v)	befestigen	Topic 4
audience (n)	Zuhörer	Topic 2
availability (n)	Verfügbarkeit	Topic 1
available (a)	verfügbar	Topics 1,3

back and forth (adv)	hin und zurück	Topic 4
bar (n)	Stab, Stange	Topic 2
basically (adv)	grundsätzlich, im Grunde genommen	Topic 2
bay (n)	Bucht	Topic 4
be concerned with something	mit etwas beschäftigt sein	Topic 1
be exposed to something	etwas ausgesetzt sein	Topic 2
be responsible for	verantwortlich sein	Topic 1
be stuck (v)	steckenbleiben	Topic 3
be subjected to something	etwas unterliegen	Topics 2,4
beam (n)	Balken, Träger	Topic 3
beam bridge (n)	Balkenbrücke	Topic 4
bear (v)	tragen, ertragen	Topics 2,3
become (v)	werden	Topic 3
bedrock (n)	fester Boden	Topic 4
behind (prep)	hinter ...	Topic 4
belong to (v)	zu etwas gehören	Topic 1
below (prep)	unter ...	Topic 4
bend (v)	biegen	Topics 2,3
beneath (prep)	unter	Topics 1,4
between (prep)	zwischen ... (zwei Sachen)	Topic 4
beyond (prep)	über ... hinaus, jenseits	Topic 3
biodegradable (a)	biologisch abbaubar	Topic 2
block of flats (n)	Wohnblock	Topic 2
bore (v)	bohren	Topic 2
boundary (n)	Grenze	Topic 1
box-shaped (a)	kastenförmig	Topic 3
branch (n)	Ast	Topic 4
break (v)	brechen	Topic 2
brick (n)	Ziegelstein	Topic 1
brief (a)	ein kurzer ...	Topic 2
briefly (adv)	kurz	Topic 2
brittle (a)	brüchig	Topic 2
broad ((a)	breit	Topic 3
buckle (v)	verbeulen, knicken, nachgeben	Topic 3
build (v)	bauen	Topic 1
building (n)	Gebäude	Topic 1
building materials	Baustoffe	Topic 1
building site	Baustelle	Topic 1
bundle (n)	Bündel	Topic 3
bundle (v)	zusammenbündeln	Topic 4
cable saddle (n)	Kabelsattel	Topic 4
cable-stayed bridge (n)	Schrägkabelbrücke	Topic 4
cantilever (a)	auskragen, herausstechen	Topics 3,4
cantilever arm (n)	Kragarm, Auslegerarm	Topic 4

cantilever bridge (n)	Auslegerbrücke	Topic 4
carbon (n)	Kohle	Topic 2
carry (v)	tragen	Topic 3
carry out (v)	durchführen	Topic 1
cast in situ	vor Ort betoniert	Topic 2
cast iron (n)	Gusseisen	Topic 2
catch fire	Feuer fangen, anzünden	Topic 2
cause (n)	Ursache	Topic 1
cause (v)	verursachen	Topic 1
century (n)	Jahrhundert	Topic 3
chain (n)	Kette	Topic 4
chain of molecules	Molekularkette	Topic 1
challenge (n)	Herausforderung	Topic 1
challenge (v)	herausfordern	Topic 1
channel (n)	Kanal	Topic 4
characteristics (n)	Eigenschaften	Topic 1
check if … (v)	überprüfen ob …/ nachschauen ob…	Topic 1
chemical compounds	chemische Verbindungen	Topic 1
circular (a)	kreisförmig	Topic 3
circle (n)	Kreis	Topic 3
clay (a)	Ton, Lehm	Topic 2
coat of paint (n)	Anstrich	Topic 2
collaborate (v)	zusammenarbeiten	Topic 1
collapse (n)	Zusammensturz	Topics 1,4
collapse (v)	zusammenstürzen, abstürzen, einstürzen	Topics 1,4
column (n)	Säule, Stütze	Topic 2
commute (v)	Pendeln	Topics 1,3
commuter (n)	Pendler	Topic 1
compare (v)	vergleichen	Topic 1
complete (v)	fertigstellen	Topic 1
completion (n)	Fertigstellung	Topic 1
composite material	Baustoffverbund	Topic 1
comprehensive (a)	umfassend	Topic 3
compress (v)	zusammendrücken	Topic 2
compression (n)	Druckkraft	Topic 2
comprise of (v)	aus etwas bestehen	Topic 4
concerning (adv)	bezüglich	Topic 1
concrete (n)	Beton	Topic 1
cone (n)	Kegel, Trichter	Topic 3
conform to something	etwas entsprechen, etwas erfüllen	Topic 4
conical (a)	kegelförmig	Topic 3
consider (v)	überlegen, betrachten	Topic 1
considerable (a)	beträchtlich	Topic 3
constantly (adv)	konstant, ständig, dauerhaft	Topic 4

construction (n)	Bau	Topic 1
construct (v)	bauen	Topic 1
construction site	Baustelle	Topic 1
contain (v)	beinhalten	Topic 2
contaminated (a)	kontaminiert	Topic 1
contractor (n)	Bauunternehmer	Topic 1
core (n)	Kern	Topic 3
corrode (v)	rosten	Topic 2
corrosion (n)	Rost, Korrosion	Topic 2
corrugated metal sheet	Metallblech, Wellblech	Topic 2
cost-effective (a)	Kostengünstig	Topic 1
counteract (v)	gegensteuern	Topic 4
counterweight (n)	Gegengewicht	Topic 4
court (n)	Gerichtshof	Topic 1
crack (n)	Riss	Topic 2
crack (v)	knacken, reißen	Topic 2
crane (n)	Kran	Topic 1
cross-bracing (n)	Aussteifung, Versteifung	Topic 4
cube (n)	Würfel	Topic 3
cuboid (a)	würfelförmig	Topic 3
cuboid (n)	Quader	Topic 3
cue cards (n)	Karteikarten	Topic 2
currently (adv)	zurzeit	Topic 4
damage (n)	Schaden	Topic 1
damage (v)	schaden	Topic 1
date back (v)	aus ... (Zeit) stammen	Topic 1
dead load	Eigenlast	Topic 2
deal with (v)	sich mit etwas beschäftigen	Topic 1
debris (n)	Bauschutt	Topic 1
deck (n)	Fahrbahn, Tragfläche	Topic 4
deep (a)	tief	Topic 4
deformation	Verformung	Topic 2
degree (n)	Grad	Topic 3
deliver (v)	liefern	Topics 1,2
delivery (n)	Lieferung	Topic 1
delivery (n)	Lieferung	Topic 2
dense (a)	dicht, dick	Topics 2,3
dent (n)	Delle, Beule	Topic 2
depend on something (v)	von etwas abhängen	Topics 1,2
dependable (a)	verlässlich, betriebssicher	Topic 4
depth (n)	Tiefe	Topic 4
derive from something (v)	etwas von etwas ableiten	Topic 3
despite (adv)	trotz	Topic 3
determine (v)	feststellen	Topic 1

develop (v)	entwickeln	Topic 1
development (n)	Entwicklung	Topic 1
diagonal cross-bracing (n)	Querversteifung	Topic 4
diamond (n)	Diamant	Topic 2
disadvantage (n)	Nachteil	Topics 2,3
disaster (n)	Desaster, Katastrophe	Topic 4
discipline (n)	Fachrichtung	Topic 1
discuss (v)	besprechen	Topic 1
discussion (n)	Debatte, Diskussion	Topic 1
displace (v)	ersetzen, austauschen	Topic 2
dispose of (v)	entsorgen	Topic 1
distribute (v)	verteilen	Topic 3
divide (v)	trennen	Topic 1
downside (n)	Nachteil	Topic 2
drainage system	Abwasserkanalisation	Topic 1
drape over (v)	überhängen	Topic 4
drawback (n)	Nachteil	Topic 3
drill (v)	bohren	Topic 2
drinking water supply	Trinkwasserversorgung	Topic 1
driveway (n)	Zufahrt	Topic 2
ductile (a)	biegsam	Topic 2
ductility (n)	Biegsamkeit	Topic 2
due to (adv)	aufgrund	Topic 2
durability (n)	Widerstandsfähigkeit	Topic 1
durable (a)	langlebig, widerstandsfähig	Topic 1
earthquake (n)	Erdbeben	Topic 1
effect (n)	Einfluss	Topic 1
effectively (a)	wirksam	Topic 1
efficiency (n)	Wirksamkeit	Topic 3
elastic (a)	elastisch, nachgiebig	Topic 2
elevation (n)	Bodenerhebung	Topic 1
elevator (n)	Aufzug	Topic 3
elevator shaft (n)	Aufzugsschacht	Topic 3
emission (n)	Abgase	Topic 1
enable (v)	ermöglichen	Topic 1
ensure (v)	sicherstellen, gewährleisten	Topic 1
environment (n)	Umgebung	Topic 1
environmental impact	Umweltbeeinflussung	Topic 1
environmentally friendly	umweltfreundlich	Topic 2
envision (v)	sich vorstellen	Topic 1
equipment (n)	Ausrüstung, Geräte	Topic 3
essential (a)	ein wesentlicher ..., notwendiger ...	Topic 2
essentially (adv)	grundsätzlich	Topic 2
estimate (n)	Einschätzung	Topic 1

estimate (v)	einschätzen	Topic 1
evaluate (v)	auswerten, einschätzen	Topic 1
evaluation (n)	Auswertung, Bewertung	Topic 1
evenly (a)	gleichmäßig	Topic 3
eventually (adv)	am Ende, letzten Endes	Topic 2
evidence (n)	Beweis, Beweisstück	Topic 1
examination (n)	Untersuchung	Topic 1
examine (v)	untersuchen	Topic 1
exceed (v)	überschreiten	Topic 2
excess water	Überschusswasser	Topic 1
execute (v)	eine Aufgabe erledigen, jemanden hinrichten	Topic 1
experience (n)	Erfahrung	Topic 2
experience (v)	erfahren, erleben	Topic 2
expert witness (n)	Gerichtssachverständiger, Gutachter	Topic 1
extend (v)	verlängern	Topic 4
extension (n)	Ausweitung	Topic 1
extraordinary (a)	außergewöhnlich	Topic 4
extremely (adv)	extrem	Topic 2
facilities (n)	Einrichtungen	Topic 3
factory (n)	Fabrik	Topic 2
failure (n)	Mangel, Versagen, Fehler	Topic 1
fairly (adv)	ziemlich (im positiven Sinn)	Topic 2
faulty construction	Baumangel, fehlerhafter Bau	Topic 1
feasibility (n)	Durchführbarkeit, Machbarkeit	Topic 1
feasible (a)	durchführbar, machbar	Topics 1,3
feature (n)	Eigenschaft	Topic 2
fiberglass (n)	Glasfasern	Topic 2
figure out (v)	herausfinden	Topic 1
flammable, inflammable (a)	entzündlich	Topic 2
flood control (n)	Hochwasserschutz	Topic 1
flood hazard (n)	Überflutungsgefahr	Topic 3
flooding (n)	Überflutung	Topic 1
fluent (a)	fließend	Topic 2
flyover (n)	Überführung	Topic 1
focus on something (v)	sich auf etwas konzentrieren	Topic 1
forces (n)	Kräfte	Topic 2
fossil fuels	fossile Brennstoffe	Topic 1
foundation (n)	Fundament	Topics 1,3
framework (n)	Gerüst	Topic 3
fulfill (v)	erfüllen	Topic 1
fumes (n)	Brandgase	Topic 2
fundamental (a)	grundsätzlich, grundlegend	Topic 3
further (adv)	weiter	Topic 3
gain (v)	gewinnen	Topic 2

garden shed (n)	Gartenhütte	Topic 2
governing factor	Hauptaspekt	Topic 3
gradually (adv)	Schritt für Schritt, allmählich	Topic 3
gravel (n)	Kies	Topic 2
gravity (n)	Schwerkraft	Topic 2
gridwork (n)	Gitternetz	Topic 2
ground level (n)	Bodenhöhe, Erdgleiche	Topic 2
ground water level	Grundwasserspiegel	Topic 1
grow (v)	wachsen	Topic 1
growth (n)	Zuwachs	Topic 1
guarantee (v)	gewährleisten, garantieren, sicherstellen	Topic 1
hang (v)	hängen	Topic 4
harbor (n)	Hafen	Topic 1
harden (v)	hart werden	Topic 1
hardly any (adv)	fast keine ..., so gut wie keine ...	Topic 2
hardness (n)	Härte	Topic 2
harmful (a)	schädlich	Topic 1
hazard (n)	Risiko	Topic 1
health hazard	Gesundheitsrisiko	Topic 2
heavy (a)	schwer	Topic 2
height (n)	Höhe	Topics 3,4
high (a)	hoch	Topics 3,4
high-rise / highrise (a)	Hochbau	Topic 2
hold (v)	halten	Topic 4
hole (n)	Loch	Topic 2
hollow (a)	hohl, leer	Topic 3
humidity (n)	Feuchtigkeit	Topic 2
identify (v)	identifizieren	Topic 1
illustration (n)	Abbildung	Topic 4
impatient (a)	ungeduldig	Topic 1
improve (v)	verbessern	Topic 1
improvement (n)	Verbesserung	Topic 1
in front of (prep)	vor ...	Topic 4
in place (n)	an der Stelle	Topic 4
in safety	in Sicherheit	Topic 4
in simple terms, ...	einfach formuliert, ...	Topic 2
increase (v)	erhöhen	Topic 1
indentation (n)	Beule, Eindrückung	Topic 2
inspect (v)	inspizieren, prüfen	Topic 1
instead (adv)	stattdessen	Topic 4
instead of ... (prep)	statt ...	Topic 4
insufficient (a)	nicht ausreichend	Topic 3
insulation (n)	Isolierung	Topic 2
interpret (v)	übersetzen, deuten, erklären	Topic 1

into (prep)	in ... herein	Topic 4
introduce something (v)	etwas einführen	Topic 4
invention (n)	Entdeckung	Topic 3
investigate (v)	untersuchen, ermitteln	Topic 1
involve (v)	beinhalten, mit einbeziehen	Topic 1
inwards (adv)	nach innen	Topic 2
island (n)	Insel	Topic 4
It depends.	Es hängt davon ab. / Es kommt darauf an.	Topic 2
joints (n)	Gelenke	Topic 3
landfill (n)	Mülldeponie	Topic 1
landslide (n)	Erdrutsch	Topic 1
law enforcement officer (n)	Gesetzeshüter	Topic 1
lay (v)	legen	Topic 1
length (n)	Länge	Topic 4
lift (v)	heben, hochheben	Topics 3,4
lift (n)	Lift, Fahrstuhl	Topic 3
light, lightweight (a)	leicht	Topic 2
limit (n)	Grenzwert	Topic 1
limit (v)	begrenzen	Topic 1
line (n)	Linie	Topic 3
linear (a)	gradlinig	Topic 3
linking words (n)	Verbindungswörter	Topic 2
live load	Nutzlast	Topic 2
load bearing capacity	Tragfähigkeit	Topics 2,3
loads (n)	Lasten	Topic 2
long (a)	lang	Topic 4
loop (n)	Rundweg	Topic 4
low-rise / lowrise (a)	niedrigbau	Topic 2
lower (v)	reduzieren	Topic 3
lower in (v)	herunterlassen	Topic 2
magnificent (a)	wunderbar	Topic 1
mainland (n)	Festland	Topic 4
maintain (v)	instand halten, pflegen	Topic 1
maintenance (n)	Instandhaltung	Topic 1
major task (n)	Hauptaufgabe	Topic 1
make sure that ...	sicherstellen, sich vergewissern	Topic 1
manifest (v)	etwas aufweisen	Topic 2
manufacture (v)	herstellen	Topic 3
map out (v)	kartographieren	Topic 1
masonry walls (n)	Trockenmauerwerk	Topic 3
meanwhile (adv)	während	Topic 3
measurement (n)	Ausmessung, Maß	Topic 1
melting point (n)	Schmelzpunkt, Schmelztemperatur	Topic 2
merely (a)	lediglich	Topic 4

miscalculate (v)	falsch kalkulieren	Topic 1
miscalculation (n)	Fehlkalkulation	Topic 1
moderately (a)	mäßig	Topic 3
moldability (n)	Formbarkeit	Topic 2
monitor (v)	beobachten, überwachen	Topic 1
mortar (n)	Mörtel	Topic 1
mud (n)	Match	Topic 2
naturally (adv)	natürlich	Topic 2
neighborhood (n)	Nachbarschaft	Topic 1
nevertheless (adv)	nichtdestotrotz	Topic 4
not ... enough	nicht ... genug	Topic 2
obstacle (n)	Hindernis	Topic 4
obviously (adv)	offensichtlich	Topic 2
obviously (adv)	offensichtlich	Topic 2
occasional (a)	ein gelegentlicher ...	Topic 2
occasionally (adv)	gelegentlich	Topic 2
occupants (n)	Bewohner, Nutzer	Topic 3
off (prep)	herunter von ...	Topic 4
offer (v)	anbieten	Topic 1
operate (v)	betätigen	Topic 1
opposite (prep)	gegenüber	Topic 4
opposite (a)	gegenüberliegende	Topic 4
opposite directions	entgegengesetzte Richtungen	Topic 2
out of (prep)	aus ... heraus	Topic 4
outstretched (a)	ausgestreckt	Topic 4
overhanging (a)	überhängend	Topic 4
oversee (v)	beaufsichtigen	Topic 1
ownership (n)	Besitz, Eigentum	Topic 1
particular (a)	ein spezieller ..., bestimmter ..., besonderer ...	Topic 2
particularly (adv)	besonders	Topic 2
passage (n)	Übergang	Topic 4
patience (n)	Geduld	Topic 1
pay attention to something (v)	auf etwas achtgeben, beachten	Topic 2
pencil (n)	Bleistift	Topic 4
penetrate (v)	einsickern, eindringen	Topic 2
perimeter walls	Umfassungswand	Topic 3
pier (n)	Brückenpfeiler	Topic 4
pile (n)	Pfahl, Pfosten	Topic 2
pipeline (n)	Rohrleitung	Topic 1
place (v)	hinstellen, legen	Topic 1
plastic (a)	plastisch, formbar	Topic 2
plastic (n)	Kunststoff	Topic 1
population (n)	Bevölkerung	Topic 1
pose a risk (v)	Risiko darstellen	Topic 3

pour concrete	Beton gießen	Topic 2
pre-cast (a)	vorgefertigt	Topic 2
prefer (v)	bevorzugen	Topic 2
preferred (a)	bevorzugt	Topic 2
pressure (n)	Druck	Topic 3
prevent something from ...-ing	etwas verhindern	Topics 2,4
principles (n)	Prinzipien	Topic 4
profession (n)	Beruf	Topic 1
professional (a)	fachlich, kompetent	Topic 1
professional (n)	Expert, Fachpersonal	Topic 1
project into space (v)	ins Freie herausragen, hervorstehen	Topic 4
pronounce (v)	aussprechen	Topic 2
pronunciation (n)	Aussprache	Topic 2
proper (a)	ein angemessener ..., richtiger ...	Topic 2
properly (adv)	angemessen, richtig	Topic 2
properties (n)	Eigenschaften	Topic 1
protect (v)	schützen	Topic 1
protect against something (v)	gegen etwas schützen	Topic 2
protection (n)	Schutz	Topic 1
provide (v)	anbieten, zur Verfügung stellen	Topic 2
public transportation system	öffentliche Verkehrsmittel	Topic 1
pull apart (v)	auseinanderziehen	Topic 2
purchase (n)	Kauf	Topic 1
purchase (v)	kaufen, anschaffen	Topic 1
purification (n)	Reinigung, Klärung	Topic 1
push together (v)	zusammendrücken	Topic 2
pylon (n)	Mast	Topic 4
quite (adv)	ziemlich (neutraler Sinn)	Topic 2
railings (n)	Schutzgeländer, Gitterstab	Topic 2
railroad (n)	Bahnstrecke	Topic 1
railway (n)	Bahnstrecke	Topic 1
rather (adv)	ziemlich (im negativen Sinn)	Topic 2
reason (n)	Grund	Topic 4
reasonable (a)	angemessen, günstig, sinnvoll, vernünftig	Topics 2, 3
recently (adv)	kürzlich	Topic 2
rectangle (n)	Viereck	Topic 3
rectangular (a)	viereckig	Topic 3
reduce (v)	reduzieren	Topic 1
reinforced concrete (n)	Stahlbeton	Topics 1,2
release (v)	freisetzen	Topic 2
remote-controlled (a)	ferngesteuert	Topic 2
renewable energy resources	erneuerbare Energien	Topic 1
rent out (v)	vermieten	Topic 3
require (v)	erfordern	Topic 1

requirement (n)	Forderung, Anforderung	Topic 1
research (n)	Forschung	Topic 1
research (v)	forschen, nachforschen	Topic 1
resemble (v)	ähneln, ähnlich aussehen wie ...	Topic 3
resist (v)	standhalten, widerstehen	Topics 2,4
resolve (v)	lösen	Topic 1
rest on something (v)	auf etwas ruhen, liegen	Topic 4
result in something (v)	zu etwas führen	Topic 2
retain (v)	behalten, nicht verlieren	Topic 2
reverse (a)	umgekehrt	Topic 1
rigid (a)	steif	Topic 4
roadway (n)	Fahrbahn	Topic 4
rock (n)	Fels	Topic 1
rod (n)	Stab, Stange	Topic 2
roller shutters (n)	Rollladen	Topic 2
rope (n)	Seil	Topic 4
rot (v)	verrotten	Topic 2
rubber (n)	Gummi	Topic 2
rust (v)	rosten	Topic 2
satellite imagery (n)	Satellitenbilder	Topic 1
scrap (n)	Schrott	Topic 1
scratching ... (n)	Kratz-...	Topic 2
secure (v)	sichern	Topic 4
semicircular (a)	halbkreisförmig	Topic 3
settle (v)	sich senken, sacken	Topic 2
settlement (n)	Bodensenkung, Bodensetzung	Topic 2
severe (a)	schwerwiegend	Topic 2
sewage system (n)	Kanalisation	Topic 1
shape (n)	Form	Topic 1
shape (v)	formen	Topic 1
shear, shearing (n)	Scherkraft	Topic 2
signpost (v)	mit Wegweisern versehen	Topic 2
sink (v)	sich senken, sacken	Topic 2
skeleton (n)	Gerüst	Topic 3
skyscraper (n)	Wolkenkratzer	Topic 2
slide (v)	gleiten	Topic 2
soil (n)	Erdboden	Topic 1
solution (n)	Lösung	Topic 1
solve (v)	lösen	Topic 1
sophisticated (a)	hochentwickelt, fortgeschritten	Topic 1
span (n)	Stützweite, Abstand	Topic 4
span (v)	sich über etwas erstrecken, überbrücken, umfassen	Topic 4
sphere (n)	Kugel	Topic 3
spherical (a)	kugelförmig	Topic 3

spin (v)	spinnen	Topic 4
spread apart (v)	sich ausdehnen, sich verbreiten	Topic 4
square (a)	quadratförmig	Topic 3
square (n)	Quadrat	Topic 3
squeeze together (v)	zusammendrücken	Topic 2
stainless steel (n)	Edelstahl	Topic 2
stairway (n)	Treppenhaus	Topic 3
stamina (n)	Durchhaltevermögen	Topic 1
state-of-the-art (a)	hochmodern, auf dem neusten Stand	Topic 1
stay (n)	Spannseil	Topic 4
steel (n)	Stahl	Topic 1
steel cable (n)	Stahlkabel	Topic 4
strand (n)	Strang, Faden	Topic 4
strengthen (v)	stärken, verstärken	Topic 4
stretch (v)	auseinanderziehen	Topic 2
study (v)	etwas untersuchen, näher betrachten	Topic 1
sturdy (a)	robust, stabil	Topics 1, 4
subcontractor (n)	Zulieferer, Subunternehmer	Topic 1
substructure (n)	Unterbau, Fundamentkonstruktion	Topic 2
subway (n)	U-Bahn	Topic 1
sudden (a)	ein plötzlicher ...	Topic 2
suddenly (adv)	plötzlich	Topic 2
suggest (v)	vorschlagen	Topic 1
suggestion (n)	Vorschlag	Topic 1
suitable (a)	geeignet	Topic 1
summary (n)	Schluss, abschließende Worte	Topic 2
summit (n)	Spitze	Topic 3
superstructure (n)	Oberbau	Topic 2
supplier (n)	Zulieferer	Topic 1
support (v)	unterstützen	Topic 1
supply (v)	beliefern	Topic 1
surface (n)	Oberfläche	Topic 1
surroundings (n)	Umgebung	Topic 1
survey (n)	Überprüfung, Gutachten, Vermessung	Topic 1
survey (v)	prüfen, vermessen	Topic 1
surveying (n)	Vermessung	Topic 1
suspend (v)	anhängen, aufheben	Topic 4
suspension bridge (n)	Hängebrücke	Topic 4
sustainability (n)	Nachhaltigkeit	Topic 1
sustainable (a)	nachhaltig	Topics 1,2
swell (v)	anschwellen	Topic 2
take into consideration	in Betracht ziehen	Topic 1
take notes (v)	Notizen machen, notieren	Topic 2
take place (v)	passieren, stattfinden	Topic 1

tap / faucet (n)	Wasserhahn	Topic 2
tensile force / tension (n)	Zugkraft	Topic 2
tension (n)	Zugkraft	Topic 2
testify (v)	aussagen	Topic 1
therefore (adv)	deswegen, aus diesem Grund	Topic 4
thermal load (n)	Wärmelast, Temperaturbelastung	Topic 2
thin (a)	dünn	Topics 2, 3
thin (v)	verdünnen, dünn werden	Topic 3
thorough (a)	gründlich	Topic 1
tilt (v)	neigen, kippen	Topic 3
to be able to	in der Lage sein, zu etwas fähig sein, können	Topic 2
to mold (v)	formen, in Form gießen	Topic 2
too ...	zu ...	Topic 2
torsion (n)	Verdrehung	Topic 2
towards (prep)	in Richtung ...	Topic 4
tower (n)	Turm	Topic 4
toxic (a)	giftig	Topic 2
trace (n)	Spur	Topic 2
trace back (v)	zurückverfolgen	Topic 1
transition (n)	Übergang	Topic 3
treat (v)	behandeln	Topic 1
treatment (n)	Behandlung	Topic 1
tremors (n)	Beben, Erschütterungen	Topic 2
triangle (n)	Dreieck	Topic 3
triangular (a)	dreieckig	Topic 3
tribe (n)	Stamm	Topic 4
truck (n)	Lastwagen	Topic 1
truss (n)	Fachwerk, Ausleger	Topic 4
truss bridge (n)	Fachwerkbrücke	Topic 4
tube (n)	Röhre	Topic 3
twist (v)	verdrehen	Topic 2
two-storey (a)	zweistöckig	Topic 2
underground (a)	unterirdisch	Topic 1
underneath (adv)	darunter	Topic 4
unevenly (a)	ungleichmäßig	Topic 3
unfortunately (adv)	leider, bedauerlicherweise	Topic 2
unimaginable (a)	unvorstellbar	Topic 1
unique (a)	einzigartig	Topic 4
unpredictable (a)	unberechenbar	Topics 2,3
upper floors	höhere Stockwerke	Topic 3
utility room (n)	Hauswirtschaftsraum, Energieversorgungsraum	Topic 3
utilize (v)	verwenden	Topic 3
valley (n)	Tal	Topic 4
value (n)	Wert	Topic 2

various (a)	zahlreich	Topic 1
vehicle (n)	Fahrzeug	Topic 1
warn (v)	warnen	Topic 2
warning (n)	Warnung	Topic 2
waste management (n)	Müllentsorgung	Topic 1
waste water	Abwasser	Topic 1
water treatment plant	Kläranlage	Topic 1
weigh (v)	wiegen	Topics 2,3
weight (n)	Gewicht	Topics 2,3
What a pity!	Wirklich schade!	Topic 2
wide (a)	breit	Topics 3,4
widespread (a)	umfassend, weitverbreitet	Topic 1
width (n)	Breite	Topics 3,4
willing (a)	bereit, willens sein	Topic 1
willingness (n)	Bereitschaft (um etwas zu machen)	Topic 1
wind eddies (n)	Windwirbel	Topic 4
wire (n)	Draht	Topic 4
withstand (v)	standhalten, widerstehen	Topic 2
wood / timber (n)	Holz	Topic 2
yield (v)	nachgeben	Topic 2
yield point (n)	Dehngrenze	Topic 2
yield strength (n)	Formänderungsfestigkeit	Topic 2